Jiwu Zhao

Automatic Subspace Clustering

Jiwu Zhao

Automatic Subspace Clustering

for High-Dimensional Data

Südwestdeutscher Verlag für Hochschulschriften

Impressum / Imprint
Bibliografische Information der Deutschen Nationalbibliothek: Die Deutsche Nationalbibliothek verzeichnet diese Publikation in der Deutschen Nationalbibliografie; detaillierte bibliografische Daten sind im Internet über http://dnb.d-nb.de abrufbar.
Alle in diesem Buch genannten Marken und Produktnamen unterliegen warenzeichen-, marken- oder patentrechtlichem Schutz bzw. sind Warenzeichen oder eingetragene Warenzeichen der jeweiligen Inhaber. Die Wiedergabe von Marken, Produktnamen, Gebrauchsnamen, Handelsnamen, Warenbezeichnungen u.s.w. in diesem Werk berechtigt auch ohne besondere Kennzeichnung nicht zu der Annahme, dass solche Namen im Sinne der Warenzeichen- und Markenschutzgesetzgebung als frei zu betrachten wären und daher von jedermann benutzt werden dürften.

Bibliographic information published by the Deutsche Nationalbibliothek: The Deutsche Nationalbibliothek lists this publication in the Deutsche Nationalbibliografie; detailed bibliographic data are available in the Internet at http://dnb.d-nb.de.
Any brand names and product names mentioned in this book are subject to trademark, brand or patent protection and are trademarks or registered trademarks of their respective holders. The use of brand names, product names, common names, trade names, product descriptions etc. even without a particular marking in this works is in no way to be construed to mean that such names may be regarded as unrestricted in respect of trademark and brand protection legislation and could thus be used by anyone.

Coverbild / Cover image: www.ingimage.com

Verlag / Publisher:
Südwestdeutscher Verlag für Hochschulschriften
ist ein Imprint der / is a trademark of
OmniScriptum GmbH & Co. KG
Heinrich-Böcking-Str. 6-8, 66121 Saarbrücken, Deutschland / Germany
Email: info@svh-verlag.de

Herstellung: siehe letzte Seite /
Printed at: see last page
ISBN: 978-3-8381-3830-5

Zugl. / Approved by: Düsseldorf, Heinrich Heine University, Uni, Diss., 2013

Copyright © 2014 OmniScriptum GmbH & Co. KG
Alle Rechte vorbehalten. / All rights reserved. Saarbrücken 2014

Dedicated to

Sviatlana & Lilu

CONTENTS

1 Introduction & Background   **1**

2 Related work   **9**
    2.1 Traditional clustering algorithms 9
    2.2 Subspace clustering algorithms 16
    2.3 Problem & Motivation 23

3 Subspace clustering methods   **27**
    3.1 Definitions 27
       3.1.1 Data & Data set 27
       3.1.2 Subspace clusters 28
       3.1.3 Distance & Density 30
    3.2 Subspace Clustering with the Gravitation Function (SUGRA) . . 33
       3.2.1 Basic ideas of SUGRA 33
       3.2.2 Algorithm of SUGRA 38
    3.3 Automatic Subspace Clustering with the Distance -Density Function (ASCDD) 45
       3.3.1 Motivation of ASCDD 45
       3.3.2 Distance-Density function 46
       3.3.3 Find potential subspaces with entropy 50
       3.3.4 Exploring clusters 56
       3.3.5 Algorithm of ASCDD 63
    3.4 Summary 66

CONTENTS

4 Discussion & Comparison   **67**
- 4.1 Discussion about SUGRA 67
  - 4.1.1 Parameter choice 67
  - 4.1.2 Data scale 68
  - 4.1.3 Cluster shapes 69
- 4.2 Discussion about ASCDD 70
  - 4.2.1 Parameter choice 70
  - 4.2.2 Cluster shapes 73
  - 4.2.3 Time complexity 75
- 4.3 Comparison 76
  - 4.3.1 SUGRA versus ASCDD 76
  - 4.3.2 SUGRA versus CLIQUE 77
  - 4.3.3 ASCDD versus DENCLUE 79
  - 4.3.4 ASCDD versus ENCLUS 81
- 4.4 Summary 83

5 Empirical experiments   **85**
- 5.1 Experiments with SUGRA 86
  - 5.1.1 Synthetic data 86
  - 5.1.2 Real data 89
- 5.2 Experiments on ASCDD 92
  - 5.2.1 Synthetic Data 92
  - 5.2.2 Real Data 98

6 Conclusion   **103**

7 Appendixes   **105**
- 7.1 Appendix A 105

CONTENTS

References   **109**

List of Figures   **123**

List of Tables   **125**

Index   **127**

CONTENTS

1
INTRODUCTION & BACKGROUND

"One man's noise can be another man's music."[1]

It is nowadays uncomplicated to gather real-time bulk data with high-speed, high-capacity and low-priced data storage devices in various domains, e.g. economics, meteorology, genetics, and security. However, the huge bulk of data is usually stored as unanalyzed raw data, whose meaning or implications are difficult to be revealed. In order to extract the significance of original data and to utilize useful information for further analysis, it is necessary to discover unknown or hidden information from the raw data.

Data mining is a process of discovering and exploiting hidden information in data and converting the information more comprehensibly for further applications. Data mining involves many tasks for various requirements. A few common tasks are introduced here shortly:

Classification identifies categories for new objects by analyzing the existing categories of known data.

Regression analysis is a statistical method for estimating a model that optimally fits data and investigating relationships between variables.

---
[1][Air 57]

Association rule mining is a method for exploring interesting relations between objects.

Anomaly detection tries to find outliers, which do not have normal patterns compared with other objects.

Clustering discovers groups of objects with similar properties or structures.

Clustering is one of the core tasks in data mining because it is the foundation for many other data mining tasks, such as classification, association rule mining and anomaly detection. It is also commonly used in many domains such as marketing, biology, medicine, World Wide Web, machine learning and information retrieval.

The main purpose of a clustering task is to divide the objects in a data set into groups (clusters), so that according to some principle the objects in the same cluster are similar. Meanwhile, the ones from different clusters are dissimilar. This is the general principle for clustering. The definitions of clusters are usually based on similarities defined by various clustering algorithms. However, the explanations and definitions of the similarity between objects vary with clustering algorithms.

Traditional clustering algorithms consider all dimensions of a data set as a unity for seeking possible clusters. This is mainly meaningful for low-dimensional data. However, as the number of dimensions increases, the traditional clustering methods may face some problems.

One problem is that clusters may not exist in the entire space, but in some projections of the dimensions. This often happens in high-dimensional data sets. Since many dimensions are often irrelevant in high-dimensional data, the irrelevant dimensions can confuse traditional clustering algorithms with hidden clusters in noise [Pars 04].

Another issue when applying traditional clustering methods to high-dimensional data arises from the *"curse of dimensionality"* [Bell 03, Beye 99]. The phenomenon of the "curse of dimensionality" shows that objects are getting increasingly sparse and dissimilar as the dimensionality increases; meanwhile, the distance between two objects converges $\left(\frac{dist_{\min}}{dist_{\max}} \xrightarrow{dim \to \infty} 1\right)$ and consequently many algorithms may work inefficiently.

An example illustrates the phenomenon of "curse of dimensionality" in figure 1.1, where the figures (a), (b) and (c) illustrate objects that spread out in one, two and three dimensions, where the objects are enclosed with unit bins in diverse dimensions. It shows that the number of objects contained in a one unit bin decreases as the number of dimensions increases. In some sense, a high-dimensional unit bin can be said to be "sparser" than a low-dimensional unit bin. Therefore, the distances between objects in high dimensions tend to be more "equal" than the distances between objects in low dimensions. In this situation, the traditional clustering algorithms can be inapplicable for high-dimensional data sets.

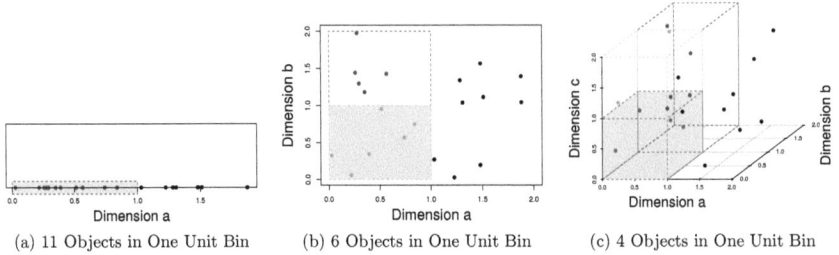

(a) 11 Objects in One Unit Bin (b) 6 Objects in One Unit Bin (c) 4 Objects in One Unit Bin

Figure 1.1: An example of "curse of dimensionality" [Pars 04]

Unlike traditional clustering methods, which search clusters only in the entire space of a data set, *subspace clustering* methods focus on seeking clusters

1. INTRODUCTION & BACKGROUND

in particular projections of dimensions (*subspaces*). A subspace cluster can be found in arbitrary subspaces rather than only in the entire space. In other words, only the significant subspaces are found with clusters by subspace clustering algorithms.

Figure 1.2 shows an example of a three dimensional data set. The objects are mixed with interlaced patterns. It is difficult to explore correct clusters by applying a traditional clustering method only in the three dimensional space, because the dissimilarities between clusters are not big enough to separate them. If the objects are projected into two dimensional subspaces, then one cluster appears much clearly. For example, the objects of cluster 1 are closer to each other than the objects of cluster 2 or 3 in subspace $\{x, y\}$. Indeed, cluster 1 can be easily found in $\{x, y\}$. It implicates that the subspace $\{x, y\}$ has significant relationship with cluster 1. Similarly, cluster 2 and cluster 3 can be found in $\{x, z\}$ and $\{y, z\}$ respectively.

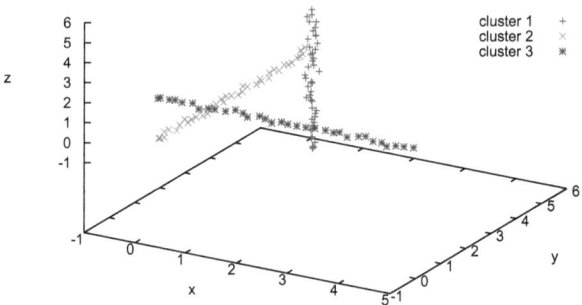

Figure 1.2: An example of subspace clusters

Subspace clustering can be applied in many domains. One prominent example is gene analysis, the important gene expression information is saved in

DNA microarray data, where the *expression level* of large number of genes is usually measured under many different conditions. Each condition corresponds to a dimension. One challenging work is to explore patterns from the data. For example, checking whether homogeneous expression levels indicate a common function or searching genetic relationships. In such searching tasks with massive high-dimensional data sets, subspace clustering techniques can surely play an important role.

Another interesting example is face recognition, which can be used in security systems, human-machine interaction and so on. It is a challenging area in pattern recognition, because human faces are generally similar. It needs many features to distinguish faces. Moreover, many factors can result in difficulties for the recognition, such as pose, illumination, facial expression and cover. The features with different conditions are usually saved as a high-dimensional data set. A common task is to check whether the features of two faces are identical. Subspace clustering can be definitely used for such applications.

There are a large number of published studies about various clustering techniques, e.g. density-based, partition-based, hierarchy-based [Han 06]. Why are there so many clustering algorithms? In [Esti 02], the author points out that the notion of "cluster" cannot be precisely defined, because "clusters are in part in the eye of the beholder". In other words, the researchers try to define the principles of clusters. These principles decide the similarity and dissimilarity of objects. The principles of various methods are so different, so that the clustering results may not be the same with various algorithms. For example, some clustering algorithms allow that one object belongs to only one cluster, whereas other clustering algorithms enable that an object assigns to many clusters. It is also possible that one algorithm's noise object can be another one's cluster object.

1. INTRODUCTION & BACKGROUND

One of the most challenging tasks for clustering algorithms is to assign objects on the "edge" of clusters or "between" two and more clusters. The objects at these special places can indicate forms of clusters, so assigning these objects can result in big or small clusters. However, the assignment of these objects depends strongly on the definition of similarity and also on the setting of parameters in each clustering algorithm.

Choosing parameters is important for many clustering algorithms because adjusting the parameters can change the clustering results. In many subspace clustering algorithms, parameters are usually required for both clusters and subspaces detection. However, a major problem is that most parameters can be difficult to determine, especially if a data set has unknown information or complicated types of data. The clustering algorithms can be even inapplicable for some situations when their parameters are hard to choose.

The main aim of our study is to develop subspace clustering methods for automatically clustering high-dimensional data. In order to achieve this purpose, we try to reduce parameters and to make parameters easily determinable. This dissertation summarizes mainly two of our studies, SUGRA (Subspace Clustering with the Gravitation Function) [Zhao 10a] and ASCDD (Automatic Subspace Clustering with the Distance -Density Function)[Zhao 12, Zhao 13].

SUGRA is an automatic density-based subspace clustering algorithm. It applies a mathematical property to separate non-cluster objects from others in a simple way. It enables clustering without giving complex parameters.

The other method ASCDD is a development of SUGRA. ASCDD is also a density-based subspace clustering algorithm, which applies very different techniques as SUGRA in searching for clusters and subspaces. The algorithm uses one parameter that can be simply determined.

The overall structure of the dissertation takes the form of following chapters, including this introductory chapter. Chapter 2 begins by presenting related research in the areas of clustering and subspace clustering. We introduce here the problems of existing approaches and motivations of our studies. Chapter 3 gives the definitions used for this study and details of our two subspace clustering algorithms. Chapter 4 focuses on discussing some issues of our studies and comparisons to other subspace clustering methods. The next chapter 5 presents experimental studies for verifying the proposed methods. Finally, chapter 6 contains conclusions together with some ideas for further work.

1. Introduction & Background

2
RELATED WORK

In this chapter, we present some famous traditional clustering algorithms and subspace clustering algorithms with their brilliant conceptions and also their drawbacks. Finally, we elaborate the motivation and targets of our studies.

2.1 Traditional clustering algorithms

The traditional clustering algorithms denote the clustering algorithms that are not used for the purpose of subspace clustering. The traditional clustering algorithms use different techniques, which can be generally categorized as density-based, statistics-based, hierarchy-based and partition-based clustering methods [Han 06]. We will introduce here some well-known traditional clustering algorithms.

Density-based clustering methods calculate the density values for objects. The objects in a cluster are usually in the area with high density. Meanwhile, the objects with low density are considered to be non-cluster objects.

DBSCAN (Density-Based Spatial Clustering of Applications with Noise) [Este 96] is a density-based clustering algorithm that finds clusters by estimating the density distribution of corresponding objects.

2. RELATED WORK

DBSCAN is based on the following definitions. A core object has more objects than $minPts$ (the minimum number of objects for forming a cluster) in its ε-neighborhood, which is the set of objects with distances to the core object smaller than ε. The objects in the ε-neighborhood of a core object are directly density-reachable to this core object. Two objects are density-reachable, if there is a chain of objects that are directly density-reachable between these two objects. Furthermore, two objects are density-connected, if they are density-reachable through another object.

Searching a cluster in DBSCAN starts from a core object. All objects that are density-connected with the start object are added to this cluster. The cluster is expanded by adding new objects that are density-connected to any object in the same cluster.

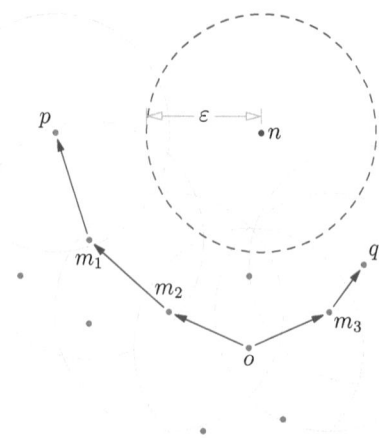

Figure 2.1: DBSCAN with $minPts = 5$

Figure 2.1 shows an example of DBSCAN. By choosing $MinPts = 5$, o is a core object, since o has the ε-neighborhood with more than 5 objects. Objects p

2.1 TRADITIONAL CLUSTERING ALGORITHMS

and q are density-reachable through a chain of directly density-reachable objects $\{m_1, m_2, o, m_3\}$ thus p, q are density-connected and belong to the same cluster. The object n is a noise object, which is not density-connected to any cluster object.

DBSCAN has the following main advantages:

- DBSCAN can find arbitrarily shaped clusters, especially with concave forms.

- The clustering process can start from any core object. It is not necessary to estimate the number of clusters.

However, DBSCAN has some disadvantages as follows:

- Because of the "curse of dimensionality"[Bell 03, Beye 99], the Euclidean distance as the metric used in DBSCAN is not suitable for high-dimensional data sets.

- The setting of the two important parameters ε and $minPts$ can be difficult for a data set with unknown information.

Statistics-based clustering methods are usually based on statistical distribution models. With the strong theoretical foundation it can yield not only clusters, but also statistical properties for a data set, e.g. dependence and correlation. If objects belong to the same distribution, they belong usually to the same cluster.

It is necessary to select appropriate statistical distribution models for real data sets. However, choosing a statistical distribution model is sometimes complicated, because not all data sets have the same distribution.

2. RELATED WORK

A famous statistical method is EM (Expectation-Maximization) algorithm [Demp 77], which tries to find the *maximum a posteriori probability* or *maximum likelihood* with iterations. The parameters of the statistical models that fit to data sets are estimated iteratively.

DENCLUE (Density-based clustering) [Hinn 98] is a statistics-based clustering algorithm that applies the *Gaussian kernel function* for estimating density values of objects. The density function for an object o in a data set with N objects is defined as:

$$f(o) = \sum_{i=1}^{N} e^{-\frac{d(o,o_i)}{2\sigma^2}} \quad (2.1)$$

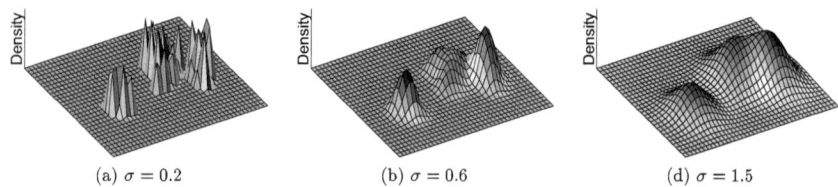

(a) $\sigma = 0.2$ (b) $\sigma = 0.6$ (d) $\sigma = 1.5$

Figure 2.2: Density values of DENCLUE with different σ [Hinn 98]

The densities of objects can be calculated using the density function. The *standard deviation* σ as a parameter indicates the influence of an object on other objects. The value of σ decides also the density divergence between cluster objects and outliers. As shown in figure 2.2, a small σ results in a "sharp" form of density values.

Another important parameter required by DENCLUE is ξ, which is the minimal density required for forming a cluster. The value of ξ determines the size of the clusters. Figure 2.3 shows the clustering results with two different values of the parameter ξ. More objects are gathered into a cluster with a small ξ than with a big ξ.

2.1 TRADITIONAL CLUSTERING ALGORITHMS

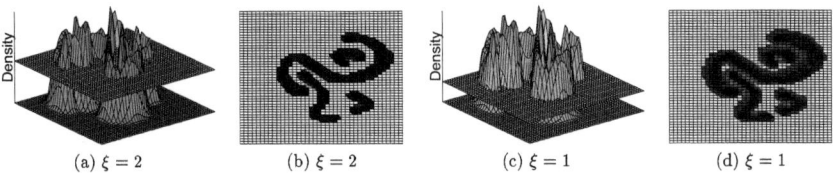

(a) $\xi = 2$ (b) $\xi = 2$ (c) $\xi = 1$ (d) $\xi = 1$

Figure 2.3: Clustering results of DENCLUE with different ξ [Hinn 98]

DENCLUE applies a *hill-climbing* procedure to find firstly objects with local maximal density (density-attractors). Then the objects are explored as a cluster when their density values exceed the minimal density ξ and meanwhile the objects are density-attracted by a density-attractor.

DENCLUE has some advantages and drawbacks.

Main advantages:

- The density values of objects show the areas of possible clusters and outliers clearly.
- It works efficiently for data sets with many outliers.
- It can be applied to find clusters with arbitrary shapes.

Some drawbacks:

- The method requires that the objects have a Gaussian distribution. However, not all data sets have a Gaussian distribution.
- It needs a careful determination of the parameters ξ and σ, because the choice of the parameters may significantly influence the clustering results.

DENCLUE 2.0 [Hinn 07] improves mainly the hill-climbing procedure of DENCLUE. Similarly, DENCLUE 2.0 depends also on the Gaussian kernel function, which means it is still necessary to estimate the parameters σ and ξ in the algorithm. In its new hill-climbing procedure two extra parameters, the iteration threshold and the percentage of the largest posteriors, are also required in DENCLUE 2.0. Both DENCLUE and DENCLUE 2.0 are not designed for high-dimensional subspace clustering.

Partition-based clustering methods divide objects of a data set into groups. Each group is represented by a central core, which may not belong to the data set. The members of groups and central cores are reassigned iteratively to improve clustering results.

k-Means [MacQ 67] is a famous partition-based clustering algorithm that partitions objects of a data set into k clusters, where k is an input parameter. Each cluster is represented by a centroid (mean of the cluster). Each object is assigned to a cluster whose centroid is closest to the object. After each assignment, the mean values of clusters are recalculated and the centroids are updated. Then each object is newly reassigned to the closest centroid. The algorithm finishes when the assignments no longer change.

k-Means works well on clearly separated objects in many situations. However, it has some disadvantages:

- The parameter k is difficult to be specified, especially for unknown data sets.

- It is unsuitable for searching clusters with concave shapes.

- k-Means is sensitive to outliers or noise objects, which influence substantially the mean values.

2.1 TRADITIONAL CLUSTERING ALGORITHMS

- It is inapplicable if the mean of the objects is not defined, e.g. the objects have non numerical properties.

Another similar partition-based clustering method, k-medoids [Rous 87], takes a real object (*medoid*) as the representation for a cluster. Instead of calculating the mean of a cluster, a medoid is the object with the minimal average distance to all the objects in the cluster. However, k-medoids has similar disadvantages as k-Means.

Fuzzy C-Means [Bezd 81] is similar to k-Means. However, Fuzzy C-Means assigns to each object a degree of belonging to clusters, thus objects can belong to more than one cluster.

Hierarchy-based clustering methods generate usually a dendrogram that represents a hierarchical structure of objects. Two types of hierarchy-based clustering methods exist, namely agglomerative and divisive methods, which depend on whether the hierarchy is constructed in a merging (bottom-up) or splitting (top-down) sequence.

Instead of directly finding clusters, a hierarchy-based clustering algorithm finds a hierarchy of the whole data set. The clusters can be obtained by a horizontal cut through the dendrogram at a desired dissimilarity level.

We introduce only the agglomerative methods here. If the distance between two objects or two clusters satisfies a distance criterion, they are merged into one node in the dendrogram. Suppose $dist(a, b)$ is the distance between two objects and $D(A, B)$ is the distance between two clusters A and B, the following three distance criteria are normally used:

Single-Link $\quad D(A, B) = \min_{a \in A, b \in B} dist(a, b)$ [Snea 57]

Complete-Link $D(A,B) = \max\limits_{a \in A, b \in B} dist(a,b)$ [McQu 60]

Average-Link $D(A,B) = \dfrac{1}{|A||B|} \sum\limits_{a \in A, b \in B} dist(a,b)$ [Soka 58]

The hierarchy-based clustering methods suffer from the inability to make adjustments once the hierarchy is constructed. It is also problematic to decide on a dissimilarity level for clustering, because choosing a parameter for this purpose is difficult.

2.2 Subspace clustering algorithms

There has been an increasing amount of literature on subspace clustering in recent years. Many subspace clustering algorithms are derived from the traditional clustering techniques. In contrast to the traditional clustering algorithms, which search clusters in the entire space, the main task of subspace clustering approaches is the detection of clusters in subspaces.

Surveys conducted by [Pars 04] and [Krie 09] have divided subspace clustering algorithms into two categories according to the searching sequence of subspace: *top-down* and *bottom-up*.

- Top-down methods (e.g. PROCLUS [Agga 99], ORCLUS [Agga 00], FINDIT [Woo 04], σ-Clusters[Yang 02], COSA [Frie 04]) search clusters from partitions of objects and improve the clustering results iteratively.

- Bottom-up methods (e.g. CLIQUE [Agra 98], ENCLUS [Chen 99], MAFIA [Goil 99], CBF [Chan 02], DOC [Proc 02], CLTree [Liu 00]) find firstly clusters in low-dimensional subspaces, and then expand the search into

2.2 SUBSPACE CLUSTERING ALGORITHMS

higher dimensions in order to find all possible high-dimensional subspace clusters.

Most subspace clustering methods apply a *downward-closure* (*monotonicity*) criterion, which is described as follows:

Proposition 1 (Downward-closure [Agra 98]). *If a cluster C exists in a k-dimensional subspace S, then C is part of a cluster in a $(k-1)$-dimensional subspace S' ($S' \subseteq S$).*

The following conclusions can be obtained from the downward-closure property:

- If there is a cluster in a subspace S, then each subspace $S' \subseteq S$ contains a cluster too.

- A cluster in a subspace S' is not necessarily a cluster in a subspace $S \supset S'$.

- A set of non-cluster objects in a subspace S' is still a set of non-cluster objects in a subspace $S \supset S'$.

With the downward-closure criterion, most bottom-up subspace clustering methods search clusters from low-dimensional subspaces to high-dimensional subspaces. The clusters found in this manner have usually hypercube shapes. In order to obtain clusters with arbitrary shapes, many algorithms provide steps for merging the clusters.

Besides the above categorizations, other surveys such as [Mull 09], [Krie 09] and [Sim 12] categorize subspace clustering methods based on their features

2. RELATED WORK

and techniques generally into grid-based, density-based and partition-based approaches. The top-down subspace clustering approaches are actually extensions of partition-based approaches, whereas grid-based and density-based approaches use mostly the bottom-up principle. We prefer to introduce the subspace clustering approaches according to their techniques and features.

Grid-based subspace clustering methods partition the data space with crossed grids and generate cells. A cell with a significant number of objects is considered dense and the objects inside are selected for forming subspace clusters. The high-dimensional subspace clusters are usually generated by combinations of low-dimensional subspace clusters according to the bottom-up principle.

CLIQUE (Automatic subspace clustering of high dimensional data for data mining applications) [Agra 98] is a representative grid-based subspace clustering algorithm using the bottom-up principle. The data space is divided into cells with the crossed grids parallel to the axes. A cell is considered as dense, if the proportion of the number of contained objects to the total number of objects is larger than a density threshold τ. Figure 2.4 shows an example of dense cells for CLIQUE. The total number of objects is 30. By choosing $\tau = 15\%$, we can find dense cells in the area C_1 and C_2.

CLIQUE detects first one-dimensional subspace cells and combines them for searching high-dimensional subspace cells with the downward-closure property. CLIQUE uses a greedy growth algorithm to cover the maximal adjacent dense cells in order to find clusters with any shapes.

The setting of parameters *intervals* and *position* of grids can influence the clustering results: If the intervals of grids are too large, many non-cluster objects can be included into a cluster; Contrarily, if the intervals are set too small, many real clusters are possibly separated into small ones or even disappear.

2.2 SUBSPACE CLUSTERING ALGORITHMS

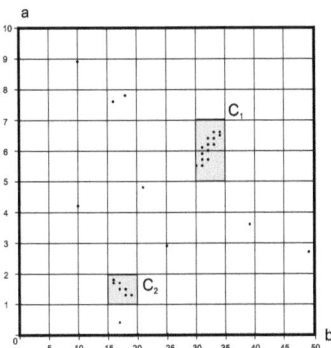

Figure 2.4: Dense units in CLIQUE [Kola 06]

ENCLUS (Entropy-based subspace clustering for mining numerical data) [Chen 99] is an extension of CLIQUE. ENCLUS tries to use three criteria: high coverage, high density and dimensional correlation for discovering subspaces with possible "good clusters". Entropy is used by ENCLUS as the metric for executing these criteria, namely the entropy values are calculated for detecting potential subspaces with clusters.

$H(X)$ is defined as the entropy of a variable X. The calculation of $H(X)$ requires a probability that is calculated as follows: Each dimension is divided into cells with equal length, and the probability is then defined as the proportion of objects contained in a cell to all objects.

ENCLUS concentrates mainly on finding interesting subspaces. The following conclusions are important for searching the interesting subspaces:

- The entropy decreases as the *coverage* increases, where coverage is the percentage of data covered by all dense units.

- The entropy decreases as the density of the dense units increases.

- A larger *interest* indicates the higher correlation between subspaces, where the interest of subspaces $X_1, \ldots, X_n$ is defined as

$$interest(\{X_1, \ldots, X_n\}) = \sum_{i=1}^{n} H(X_i) - H(X_1, \ldots, X_n) \quad (2.2)$$

Generally, a subspace with clusters has lower entropy than a subspace without clusters. ENCLUS searches for high-dimensional interesting subspaces through *interest gain*, which is defined as follows.

$$\begin{aligned}
& interest\_gain(\{X_1, \ldots, X_n\}) \\
= \; & interest(\{X_1, \ldots, X_n\}) - \\
& \max_i \{interest(\{X_1, \ldots, X_n\} - \{X_i\})\}
\end{aligned} \quad (2.3)$$

The subspaces with the entropy exceeding ω and the interest gain larger than ϵ' are considered interesting.

After detecting all possible subspace candidates, the clustering process of ENCLUS on these possible subspace candidates is the same as the process of CLIQUE. Although ENCLUS suggests a way of searching significant subspaces, it has still the same drawbacks as CLIQUE.

CLIQUE has many other extensions. For instance, MAFIA [Goil 99] uses adaptive grids to improve quality of clustering results. nCluster [Liu 07] adapts overlapping for defining one-dimensional grids. CBF [Chan 02] tries to reduce the number of cells by optimizing the partitions based on checking the maxima and minima of subspaces.

Density-based subspace clustering methods estimate the density values of a data set. The areas with high density values are considered as candidates for clusters.

2.2 SUBSPACE CLUSTERING ALGORITHMS

SUBCLU (Density-connected subspace clustering for high-dimensional data) [Krog 04] is a subspace clustering algorithm that is based on the technique of DBSCAN [Este 96]. SUBCLU redefines the terms such as ε-Neighborhood, density-reachability and density-connectivity for high-dimensional subspaces.

Similar to DBSCAN, SUBCLU calculates the density based on the number of objects in the ε-neighborhood. A cluster in a relevant subspace satisfies two properties: The objects in a cluster are density-connected with each other; If an object is density-connected to any object of a cluster, it belongs to the cluster as well.

SUBCLU uses a greedy strategy to find clusters in subspaces. With the downward-closure criterion, it checks firstly all one-dimensional subspaces, then all clusters in $(k+1)$-dimensional subspaces are detected from k-dimensional ones. If a set of objects is a cluster in a k-dimensional subspace, SUBCLU checks with the method of DBSCAN whether the set retains a cluster in a $(k+1)$-dimensional subspace.

With the density-connected method, SUBCLU can find clusters with arbitrary shapes. The parameters ε and $minPts$ are required for detecting dense areas in the subspaces. However, it is impossible to find a global setting of these two parameters for every subspace because the distances between two objects change a lot in different subspaces, especially if the subspaces of the data set have various value ranges. Additionally, a separated setting of parameters for each subspace is also impractical.

Another subspace clustering method that applies the concept of DBSCAN is PreDeCon (Density connected clustering with local subspace preferences) [Bohm 04]. It defines a weighted Euclidean distance based on a so-called subspace preference vector. A subspace for an object is relevant if the variance of objects in the ε-neighborhood of the object is smaller than a threshold. Besides the parameters required by DBSCAN, PreDeCon needs two more parameters for computing the subspace preference.

Partition-based subspace clustering methods are derived from the traditional partition-based clustering methods like k-Means.

Typical partition-based subspace clustering methods are PROCLUS (Projected clustering algorithm) [Agga 99] and its extensions, such as ORCLUS, FINDIT. PROCLUS assigns the objects in a subspace to k clusters, which are represented by k medoids.

PROCLUS has three phases: initialization, iteration, cluster refinement. In the initialization phase, PROCLUS tries to find a good set of medoids. Through the iteration phase, the medoids are recalculated and each object is reassigned to the closest medoid. The measuring of cluster quality is based on the average distance between objects and medoids. For a set of medoids, PROCLUS chooses the associated subspaces with average distances from each medoid to a set of objects within a specific distance area smaller than the statistical expectation. The refinement computes new subspaces for medoids and reassigns objects to new medoids and finally removes outliers.

PROCLUS uses sampling of objects in order to accelerate the clustering process. However, it can cause missing clusters with a small sampling of objects. The clustering result with PROCLUS is sensitive to the input parameters such as k. Moreover, it produces usually equally sized clusters with spherical shapes.

ORCLUS [Agga 00] as an extension of PROCLUS tries to find projected subspace clusters that are not parallel to the axes. By computing the covariance matrix, subspaces are relocated with the clusters. The closest pairs of clusters with similar directions are merged. The algorithm requires parameters for the number of clusters and the size of subspaces.

FINDIT [Woo 04] uses a similar concept as PROCLUS. However, FINDIT defines a dimension oriented distance for measuring medoids. The dimensions are selected through a dimension voting method. Two parameters, the minimum number of objects in a cluster and the minimum distance between two clusters, are required by FINDIT.

2.3 Problem & Motivation

As shown above, the settings of parameters in various subspace clustering methods are very important for the clustering results and quality. For instance, the parameters of partition-based subspace clustering methods (e.g. the number of clusters and the position of subspaces) influence the iterations and clustering results. For the grid-based methods, the parameters (e.g. the grid interval, the dense requirement, the size of clusters) can evidently affect the quality of clusters. In addition, parameters (such as the neighborhood size, the number of objects in neighborhood) required by density-based subspace clustering algorithms play also essential roles in searching for clusters.

The key problem of these subspace clustering methods is that they suffer from serious limitations related to determination of proper values for their parameters. The important parameters cannot be easily determined, especially when it lacks information about the data set, which is a normal situation for the clustering task. In order to make the clustering task more practical, it is necessary to find a way to determine parameters easily.

Our aim is to establish subspace clustering methods that require only a small

2. RELATED WORK

number of simple parameters. The clustering process should work automatically or semi-automatically without unpredictable parameters.

SUGRA (Subspace Clustering with the Gravitation Function) [Zhao 10a] is the first subspace clustering method proposed by us. SUGRA applies a *gravitation function* for the purpose of computing the density of objects in each dimension. In SUGRA, cluster objects can be found with the following property: the cluster objects have evidently higher values of density than non-cluster objects, which have density values lower than a threshold. The threshold is close to a constant value. The clustering process works automatically without other parameter settings. SUGRA is a bottom-up subspace clustering method, which searches firstly clusters of one-dimensional subspaces and then locates high-dimensional subspace clusters by combination of low-dimensional subspace clusters.

Although SUGRA works well in many situations, the high-dimensional subspace clusters found by SUGRA have usually hypercube shapes, which is similar to other bottom-up subspace clustering algorithms. Some merging or pruning techniques may help. However, the extra pruning processes cost much run time and can not guarantee the accuracy. So searching high-dimensional subspace clusters with the combination of low-dimensional subspace clusters is not the best solution.

For the above reason, another subspace clustering method ASCDD (Automatic Subspace Clustering with the Distance-Density Function) [Zhao 12, Zhao 13] is proposed. The aim of ASCDD is to explore clusters directly in high-dimensional subspaces as well as to simplify the determination of parameters.

The density function of ASCDD is an improvement of the gravitation function in SUGRA. With the density function of ASCDD, the density values of

2.3 Problem & Motivation

objects are calculated directly in any subspace. Based on the density values, the centers of clusters can be found easily. It applies a neighborhood technique to detect clusters with any shape. ASCDD finds a cluster by expanding neighbors of an object with high density. The neighborhood expanding technique is similar to DBSCAN. However, the definition of density-connectivity and the criterion for neighborhood expansion are different from DBSCAN. The method can be applied for differently scaled data.

In order to make the clustering process as simple and accurate as possible, ASCDD needs one parameter called DDT (distance-density threshold). DDT can influence the clustering result by determining whether two objects are neighbors (in the same cluster). We choose the value of DDT within the range $(0, 1)$ in order to set this parameter easily.

The density function of ASCDD can be applied directly on any high-dimensional subspace. However, it is still necessary to find a way to choose the right subspaces with potential clusters instead of searching each subspace.

In order to find the potential subspaces, ASCDD applies entropy to detect the potential subspaces and to reduce the complexity of searching subspaces. Unlike ENCLUS which calculates the entropy with the grid-based method, ASCDD estimates the entropy with the help of its own density function. Moreover, ASCDD uses different technique from ENCLUS to search for significant subspaces in order to locate the significant candidates of subspaces efficiently and detect clusters directly from these subspace candidates.

In the next chapter, we will introduce some definitions in section 3.1 and the details of our algorithms SUGRA and ASCDD in section 3.2 and section 3.3.

3

SUBSPACE CLUSTERING METHODS

In this chapter, we introduce two subspace clustering algorithms developed by us: SUGRA (Subspace Clustering with the Gravitation Function) [Zhao 10a] and ASCDD (Automatic Subspace Clustering with the Distance -Density Function) [Zhao 12, Zhao 13].

This chapter has been divided into three parts. The first part deals with some basic subspace clustering definitions. The following two parts describe the ideas and processes of SUGRA and ASCDD.

3.1 Definitions

3.1.1 Data & Data set

"Data are defined as series of observation, measurements, or facts in the form of numbers, words, sounds and/or images" [Robe 00]. Data can be treated as the lowest level of abstraction from which information and knowledge are derived.

In computer science, data have usually categorical or numeric types and are arranged in particular formats. Categorical data present distinct categories rather than numbers. For example, skin color and zip code are categorical data. In contrast, numeric data can be computed with various standard mathematical operations such as addition, subtraction, multiplication and division. For instance, length, weight and salary are numeric data.

A *data set* is a data-collection, which is usually structured in a tabular form that consists of rows and columns, a tree form with hierarchical structure or a graph form with interconnected nodes. Different structures are required by various applications.

In *relational databases*, a tabular form (table) is widely applied for data sets. The columns and rows in a table represent attributes and objects (tuples). All objects in a data set have usually common attributes, such as color, price, length etc. The attributes are also considered as an n-dimensional space, and an object is a vector within this space.

Definition 3.1. *A data set could be considered as a pair:* $(\mathcal{A}, \mathcal{O})$*, where $\mathcal{A}$ is a set of all attributes (dimensions):*

$$\mathcal{A} = \{a_1, a_2, \ldots\} \tag{3.1}$$

and $\mathcal{O}$ is a set of all objects:

$$\mathcal{O} = \{o_1, o_2, \ldots\} \tag{3.2}$$

$o_i^{a_m}$ denotes the value of an object o_i on dimension a_m.

A table structure of a data set $(\mathcal{A}, \mathcal{O})$ is shown in table 3.1.

3.1.2 Subspace clusters

We define here some concepts related to subspace clusters.

Definition 3.2 (Subspace). *A subspace $\widetilde{\mathcal{A}}$ of a data set $(\mathcal{A}, \mathcal{O})$ is a nonempty subset of $\mathcal{A}$:*

$$\widetilde{\mathcal{A}} \subseteq \mathcal{A} \text{ and } \widetilde{\mathcal{A}} \neq \emptyset \tag{3.3}$$

3.1 DEFINITIONS

$\mathcal{O}$ \ $\mathcal{A}$	a_1	a_2	a_3	$\cdots$	a_m	$\cdots$
o_1	$o_1^{a_1}$	$o_1^{a_2}$	$o_1^{a_3}$	$\cdots$	$o_1^{a_m}$	$\cdots$
o_2	$o_2^{a_1}$	$o_2^{a_2}$	$o_2^{a_3}$	$\cdots$	$o_2^{a_m}$	$\cdots$
$\vdots$			$\vdots$			
o_i	$o_i^{a_1}$	$o_i^{a_2}$	$o_i^{a_3}$	$\cdots$	$o_i^{a_m}$	$\cdots$
$\vdots$			$\vdots$			

Table 3.1: Table structure of a data set

Definition 3.3 (Subspace cluster). *Subspace clusters are the clusters that exist in subspaces of a data set. A subspace cluster S is also a data set, which can be described as follows:*

$$S = (\widetilde{\mathcal{A}}, \widetilde{\mathcal{O}}) \tag{3.4}$$

where the subspace $\widetilde{\mathcal{A}} \subseteq \mathcal{A}$ *and* $\widetilde{\mathcal{O}} \subseteq \mathcal{O}$.

A general principle applying to subspace clustering is that the objects in the same subspace cluster are more similar than the objects from different subspace clusters. However, the similarities between objects are diversely defined in different subspace clustering algorithms.

An object could belong to multiple subspace clusters in different subspaces, and a subspace can also be significant to different clusters. For example, $S_1 = (\mathcal{A}_1, \mathcal{O}_1)$ and $S_2 = (\mathcal{A}_2, \mathcal{O}_2)$ have the relations: $\mathcal{O}_1 = \mathcal{O}_2 \cup \{o\}$ and $\mathcal{A}_2 = \mathcal{A}_1 \cup \{a\}$. Should S_1 and S_2 with the small differences in the clustering result be regarded as two distinct clusters or the same cluster? In order to distinguish clusters with similar objects or subspaces and to avoid obscurity, we differentiate between diverse subspace clusters with following principles:

- According to the definition 3.3, a subspace cluster is identified by its objects and subspaces, so if $\{\mathcal{A}_1 \neq \mathcal{A}_2\}$ or $\{\mathcal{O}_1 \neq \mathcal{O}_2\} \implies S_1 \neq S_2$.

- If $\{\mathcal{A}_1 \supseteq \mathcal{A}_2 \text{ and } \mathcal{O}_1 = \mathcal{O}_2\}$ or $\{\mathcal{A}_1 = \mathcal{A}_2 \text{ and } \mathcal{O}_1 \supseteq \mathcal{O}_2\} \implies S_1 > S_2$.

- Because of the downward-closure property, if $S_1 > S_2 > \cdots$, only the largest subspace cluster S_1 is retained in the clustering results.

Definition 3.4 (Subspace clustering result). *A subspace clustering result C is a set of subspace clusters found in a data set by applying a subspace clustering algorithm, where C has the property: If $S \in C$ and $S > S' \implies S' \notin C$*

Our algorithms require the intersection of subspace clusters, which is defined as follows:

Definition 3.5 (Intersection). *Suppose $S_1 = (\mathcal{A}_1, \mathcal{O}_1)$ and $S_2 = (\mathcal{A}_2, \mathcal{O}_2)$ are two subspace clusters, the intersection of two subspace clusters is defined as follows:*

$$S_1 \cap S_2 = (\mathcal{A}_1 \cup \mathcal{A}_2, \mathcal{O}_1 \cap \mathcal{O}_2). \tag{3.5}$$

Subspace clustering is a process of discovering clusters in the relevant subspaces. However, a data set with an n-dimensional space has 2^n possible subspaces. It is unfeasible to traverse all possibilities when n is very large. So most subspace clustering methods try to optimize the subspace search to reduce the run time, which is also one of our aims.

3.1.3 Distance & Density

The *Euclidean distance* is usually applied to measure the distance between two objects in a *Euclidean space* $\mathbb{R}^n$. For two objects o_i and o_j, the Euclidean

3.1 DEFINITIONS

distance in space $\widetilde{\mathcal{A}}$ is

$$r^{\widetilde{\mathcal{A}}}_{o_i,o_j} = \left(\sum_{\forall a \in \widetilde{\mathcal{A}}} |o_i^a - o_j^a|^2 \right)^{1/2} \tag{3.6}$$

In order to unify coordinates of the data with different scales in each subspace, we apply normalized coordinates in our methods. The normalization of an object o_i in one dimension a is defined as $\bar{o}_i^a = \frac{o_i^a - min(o^a)}{max(o^a) - min(o^a)}$. Every normalized object has then a value $\bar{o}_i^a \in [0, 1]$. Since the normalization of objects will not change the clustering result, we use normalized o_i^a for each object in the remainder of the dissertation.

The "curse of dimensionality"[Bell 03, Beye 99] asserts that a distance measure such as the Euclidean distance becomes meaningless as the number of dimensions increases, because the distance between two objects converges and the difference of the maximal and minimal distances shrinks:

$$\lim_{|\mathcal{A}| \to \infty} \frac{dist_{max}}{dist_{min}} \to 1 \tag{3.7}$$

Due to the "curse of dimensionality", the Euclidean distance is unsuitable for direct clustering in high-dimensional space. We need an another way to measure the distance for subspace clustering.

If we imagine a data set as a substance that is composed of its molecules (objects), then the "substance" has density. The distribution of objects decides the local density inside the data set, which means the area with the objects close to each other has a higher local density than the area with sparsely populated objects. So we use this principle for the purpose of clustering: cluster objects have usually higher density than non-cluster objects.

3. SUBSPACE CLUSTERING METHODS

Assumption 1. *Data sets D_1 and D_2 have the same number of objects and the same ranges of values. D_1 has evenly distributed objects, whereas D_2 has clusters of objects. The comparison of D_1 and D_2 is shown in figure 3.1 (a) and (b). We assume that:*

- *The data set D_1 with evenly distributed objects has no clusters.*

- *Cluster objects in D_2 are denser than the evenly distributed objects in D_1.*

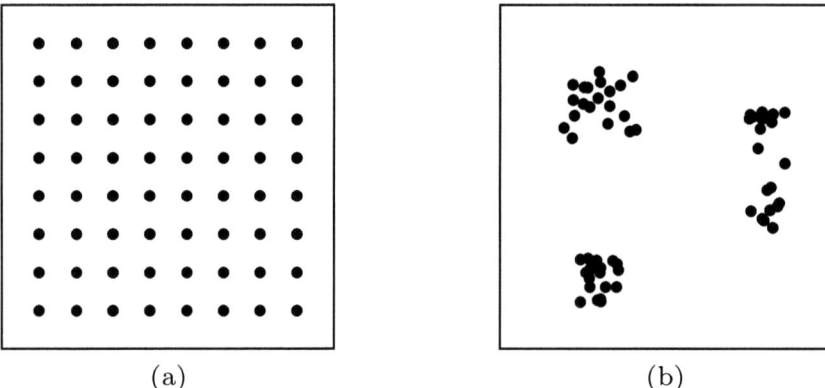

Figure 3.1: Evenly distributed objects and cluster objects

If the number of objects is very large so that we do not consider the objects at the edge, then the evenly distributed objects have the same density everywhere. There are no clusters in this situation. The density of evenly distributed objects can be considered a threshold, which is important for clustering the same number of objects.

The clusters are always associated with dense areas. In other words, a dense area can indicate a possible cluster. The definitions and calculations of density are different in diverse clustering algorithms. The density functions will be defined in the sections of the algorithms.

In the next section we will introduce the subspace clustering algorithm by using a gravitation function.

3.2 Subspace Clustering with the Gravitation Function (SUGRA)

This section will introduce one of our subspace clustering methods SUGRA (Subspace Clustering with the Gravitation Function) [Zhao 10a]. The main idea of SUGRA is to apply a gravitation function to calculate the density and to extract clusters based on the density values.

3.2.1 Basic ideas of SUGRA

Gravitation describes the force of attraction between objects with mass. *Newton's law of universal gravitation* [Newt 87] defines the gravitation G between two point masses m_1 and m_2 as follows:

$$G = \mathcal{G} \cdot \frac{m_1 m_2}{r^2} \qquad (3.8)$$

where $\mathcal{G}$ is the *gravitational constant* and r is the distance between the two point masses m_1 and m_2.

In order to apply the gravitation function on a data set for density measuring between the objects and to facilitate the calculation, we assume that:

Assumption 2 (Gravitation property in a data set).

3. SUBSPACE CLUSTERING METHODS

- The objects in a data set are attracted mutually as point masses by gravitation force.

- A single object o has the mass 1.

- The gravitational constant $\mathcal{G} = 1$.

With the above assumption, a simple gravitation function of two objects is defined here:

Definition 3.6. *Gravitation between two objects o_i and o_j on a one-dimensional subspace a is defined as follows:*

$$G^a_{o_i,o_j} = \frac{m_i m_j}{(l^a_{o_i,o_j})^2} = \frac{1}{(l^a_{o_i,o_j})^2} \tag{3.9}$$

$l^a_{o_i,o_j} = \dfrac{r^a_{o_i,o_j} \cdot (|\mathcal{O}| - 1)}{max(o^a) - min(o^a)}$ is the measurement of distance between o_i and o_j in the subspace a, where $|\mathcal{O}|$ is the number of objects and $max(o^a) - min(o^a)$ is the maximal distance of objects in subspace a. So the equation 3.9 can be transformed into:

$$G^a_{o_i,o_j} = \left(\frac{max(o^a) - min(o^a)}{r^a_{o_i,o_j} \cdot (|\mathcal{O}| - 1)} \right)^2 \tag{3.10}$$

In order to let $G^a_{o_i,o_j}$ be calculable when $r^a_{o_i,o_j} = 0$, our solution is to set $r^a_{o_i,o_j}$ to a value between 0 and the minimal positive distance in a, which is the minimal distance between the objects with a value bigger than 0. This method ensures $r^a_{o_i,o_j}$ is still the smallest distance, so that $G^a_{o_i,o_j}$ is then calculable. For example, suppose l is the minimal positive distance in a, we can set $r^a_{o_i,o_j} = l/2$ to make sure that $G^a_{o_i,o_j}$ is big enough.

3.2 SUGRA

Definition 3.7. *(Gravitation of an object) The gravitation of an object o_i in dimension a is defined as the sum of gravitation between o_i and other objects.*

$$G^a_{o_i} = \sum_{\forall j,\ j \neq i} G^a_{o_i} \qquad (3.11)$$

In a one-dimensional subspace the gravitation of an object defined in equation 3.11 has the following properties:

- Objects close to others have larger gravitation values than objects isolated from others. As shown in figure 3.2, the objects with high concentration have much higher gravitation than the evenly distributed objects.

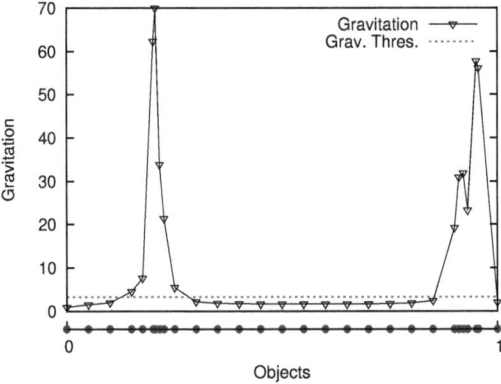

Figure 3.2: An illustration of gravitation in a one-dimensional subspace

- Evenly distributed objects do not have the same gravitation values. The center objects have larger gravitation values than the objects at the edge. Figure 3.3 illustrates an example of evenly distributed objects. The curve represents the corresponding gravitation.

3. SUBSPACE CLUSTERING METHODS

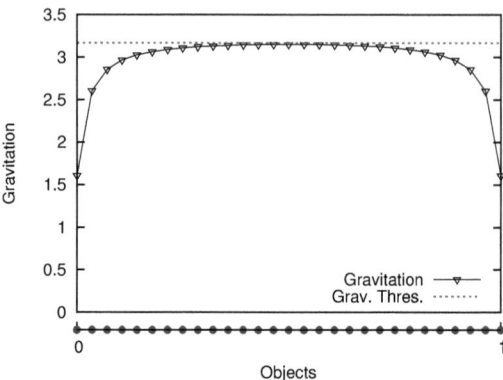

Figure 3.3: An illustration of gravitation with evenly distributed objects

As can be seen from the figure 3.2, the gravitation corresponds to the density as we discussed above. Large gravitation values indicate high densities and areas with possible clusters. Contrarily, small gravitation values indicate objects that are more sparsely distributed. These properties correspond with the definition of density. Therefore, applying gravitation for searching clusters is the main idea of SUGRA.

The gravitation values of evenly distributed objects are not the same. However, the difference is much smaller than unevenly distributed objects. For instance, the maximal difference of gravitation values in figure 3.3 is about 1.5. But the difference is about 70 in figure 3.2.

An important phenomenon is that the evenly distributed objects have gravitation values smaller than a constant value. Unevenly spaced objects have usually gravitation values larger than the same constant. The constant value is shown in figure 3.3 and figure 3.2 as a dotted line. We call this constant value the gravitation threshold.

3.2 SUGRA

Definition 3.8. *The gravitation threshold $\overline{G^a}$ of a one-dimensional subspace a is the maximal gravitation of evenly distributed objects in a.*

$\overline{G^a}$ can be estimated as follows: Suppose o_m is the middle object of evenly distributed objects o^a. As showed above, o_m has the maximal gravitation $\overline{G^a}$, which can be calculated as follows:

$$\text{Let } L := max(o^a) - min(o^a), \text{ then} \quad (3.12)$$

$$\overline{G^a} = \sum_{\forall i,\ i \neq m} \frac{L^2}{r^2_{o_m, o_i} \cdot (|\mathcal{O}| - 1)^2} \quad (3.13)$$

$$= \frac{L^2}{(|\mathcal{O}| - 1)^2} \cdot \left(\sum_{\forall i,\ i \neq m} \frac{1}{r^2_{o_m, o_i}} \right) \quad (3.14)$$

$$= \frac{L^2}{(|\mathcal{O}| - 1)^2} \cdot \left(\sum_{1 \leq n \leq \frac{|\mathcal{O}|}{2}} \frac{1}{(\frac{L}{|\mathcal{O}|-1} \cdot n)^2} \right) \cdot 2 \quad (3.15)$$

$$= 2 \cdot \left(\sum_{1 \leq n \leq \frac{|\mathcal{O}|}{2}} \frac{1}{n^2} \right) \quad (3.16)$$

Some examples of gravitation thresholds with different $|\mathcal{O}|$ are listed in the following table:

$|\mathcal{O}|$	7	22	40	50	67	100	200	1000
$\overline{G^a}$	3.02	3.20	3.24	3.25	3.26	3.27	3.28	3.287

Table 3.2: Gravitation threshold with different number of objects

As the number of objects $|\mathcal{O}|$ increases, the gravitation threshold $\overline{G^a}$ converges to a fixed value of 3.29, which can be calculated as follows:

$$\overline{G^a} = 2 \cdot \left(\sum_{1 \leq n \leq \frac{|O|}{2}} \frac{1}{n^2} \right) \xrightarrow{|O| \to \infty} 2 \cdot \frac{\pi^2}{6} = \frac{\pi^2}{3} \approx 3.29 \qquad (3.17)$$

As described above, the gravitation threshold is important for SUGRA because $\overline{G^a}$ can separate cluster objects from non-cluster objects, because the cluster objects and non-cluster objects have great differences in gravitation values. The non-cluster objects have usually smaller gravitation than $\overline{G^a}$, meanwhile the cluster objects have almost larger gravitation values than $\overline{G^a}$. The gravitation values of non-cluster and cluster objects distribute on the two sides of $\overline{G^a}$.

3.2.2 Algorithm of SUGRA

SUGRA is a bottom-up subspace clustering algorithm, which searches firstly one-dimensional subspace clusters and subsequently higher-dimensional subspace clusters based on the one-dimensional clusters. The algorithm of SUGRA consists of following steps:

1. Selection of objects (Clustering in one-dimensional subspace)

2. Selection of subspaces (Clustering in high-dimensional subspace)

3. Reduction of redundancy

Selection of objects

The main purpose of this step is selecting the cluster objects through their gravitation values for each one-dimensional subspace.

3.2 SUGRA

Algorithm 1: SUGRA (step 1): Selection of objects

Input: $(\mathcal{A}, \mathcal{O})$

Output: Set of all one-dimensional subspace clusters C

1 **foreach** $a \in \mathcal{A}$ **do**
2   sort the objects in a
3     $t = 1, O_t := \emptyset$
4   **foreach** o_i^a **do**
5   **if** $G_i^a > \overline{G^a}$ **then**
6   **if** $o_{i-1} \in O_t$ **and** $r_{o_{i-1},o_i}^a < \overline{L}$ **then**
7   set $o_i \in O_t$
8   **else**
9                 $S = (a, O_t), C = C \cup \{S\}$
10                $t = t + 1, O_t = \emptyset$
11   let $o_i \in O_t$
12   **end**
13   **end**
14 **end**
15 **end**
16 **return** C

Definition 3.9 (Cluster objects and non-cluster objects of SUGRA). *A cluster object has gravitation larger than the gravitation threshold $\overline{G^a}$. Contrarily, the objects with gravitation smaller than $\overline{G^a}$ are non-cluster objects.*

For example in figure 3.3 and figure 3.2, the objects with gravitation above the dotted line are cluster objects, whereas non-cluster objects have gravitation values below the dotted line.

The next task is to find clusters from the cluster objects. We arrange firstly the objects in one-dimensional subspaces according to their values. The objects in a one-dimensional subspace can be sorted in ascending or descending order. According to the relations of the neighboring objects we use the following principles to construct clusters from the objects:

- A cluster object o_i and the object o_{i-1} belong to the same cluster if o_{i-1} is also a cluster object and the distance between the two objects is smaller than the average distance.

- A cluster object o_i starts a new cluster in the following three situations:
  1. o_i is the first object in the search list.
  2. o_{i-1} is a non-cluster object.
  3. o_{i-1} is a cluster object and the distance between o_{i-1} and o_i is larger than the average distance.

The average distance is the distance between evenly distributed objects, which is defined as follows:

Definition 3.10 (Average distance). *The average distance $\overline{L}$ for a one-dimensional subspace a is calculated as follows:*

$$\overline{L} = \frac{|max(o^a) - min(o^a)|}{|\mathcal{O}|} \qquad (3.18)$$

As described in assumption 1, neighboring objects in a cluster should have a distance smaller than the average distance. Therefore, if the distance of two

3.2 SUGRA

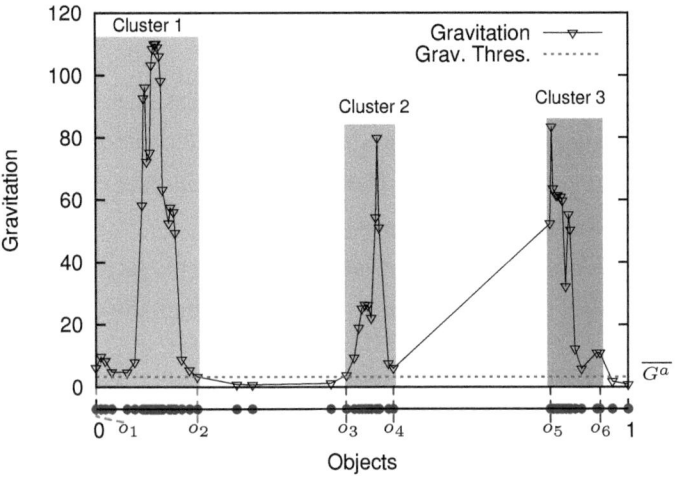

Figure 3.4: An example of clusters selection in SUGRA

neighboring cluster objects is larger than the average distance, they do not belong to the same cluster.

Figure 3.4 illustrates an example of the separation of clusters. The objects with gravitation values greater than the gravitation threshold $\overline{G^a}$ are chosen as cluster objects. Since the objects are already sorted in ascending order, the next step is to search clusters from the first to the last cluster object. For example, o_1 is the first object and a cluster object, so o_1 starts cluster 1. The following neighboring cluster objects between o_1 and o_2 are all settled in cluster 1. o_3 is assigned as the first object to cluster 2 because o_3 is the first non-cluster object after o_2. Similar to cluster 1, cluster 2 consists of the objects from o_3 to o_4. Although o_5 is the neighboring cluster object to o_4, the two objects do not belong to the same cluster. Since the distance between o_4 and o_5 is larger than the average distance (definition 3.10), o_5 starts a new cluster 3. The process stops when there is no more new cluster found in the one-dimensional subspace a. Three clusters are explored in this example.

The clusters found in this step are all one-dimensional subspace clusters. Since only the dense objects in a low-dimensional subspace could be dense in a higher-dimensional subspace, all one-dimensional subspace clusters are chosen as candidates for higher-dimensional subspaces.

The next step is the selection of subspaces, where the set of one-dimensional subspace clusters C will be applied for selecting high-dimensional subspace clusters.

Selection of subspaces

In this step, we combine low-dimensional clusters to search for higher-dimensional clusters. All one-dimensional subspace clusters are considered as original clusters. The clusters in higher-dimensional subspaces are based on the intersection (equation 3.5) of one-dimensional subspace clusters. The principle for finding higher-dimensional subspace clusters is defined as follows:

Definition 3.11. *For subspace clusters* $S_1 = (\mathcal{A}_1, \mathcal{O}_1)$ *and* $S_2 = (\mathcal{A}_2, \mathcal{O}_2)$, *if* $|\mathcal{O}_1 \cap \mathcal{O}_2| \geq N$, *then* $S_1 \cap S_2$ *is a new subspace cluster.*

N is the minimal number of objects required in a subspace cluster. In order to yield all clusters, we can set N to a small value, e.g. $N = 2$.

Figure 3.5 shows an example of SUGRA applied on a two-dimensional data set. The objects are firstly projected into each one-dimensional subspace. In each one-dimensional subspace, the objects with gravitation greater than gravitation threshold are selected as cluster objects. The one-dimensional subspace clusters are then combined and checked for finding two-dimensional subspace clusters.

3.2 SUGRA

Algorithm 2: SUGRA (step 2): Selection of subspaces
Input: The set of all one-dimensional subspace clusters C_1
Output: The set of all subspace clusters C_{all}

1   $C_{all} = C_1$
2   $dim = 2$
3   $C_{dim} = \emptyset$
4   **foreach** $S \in C_{dim-1}$ **do**
5   **while** $\exists\, S' \in C_1$ and $\mathcal{A}_{S'} \nsubseteq \mathcal{A}_S$ **do**
6          $S_{new} = S \cap S'$
7   **if** $|O^{S_{new}}| \geq 2$ **then**
8              $C_{dim} = C_{dim} \cup \{S_{new}\}$
9   **end**
10   **end**
11 **end**
12 **if** $C_{dim} \neq \emptyset$ **then**
13      $C_{all} = C_{all} \cup C_{dim}$
14   **if** $dim < |\mathcal{A}|$ **then**
15          $dim = dim + 1$
16   **go to** 3
17   **end**
18 **end**
19 **return** C_{all}

For higher-dimensional subspaces, every subspace should be checked through the intersection. This process will stop when no more new clusters are found.

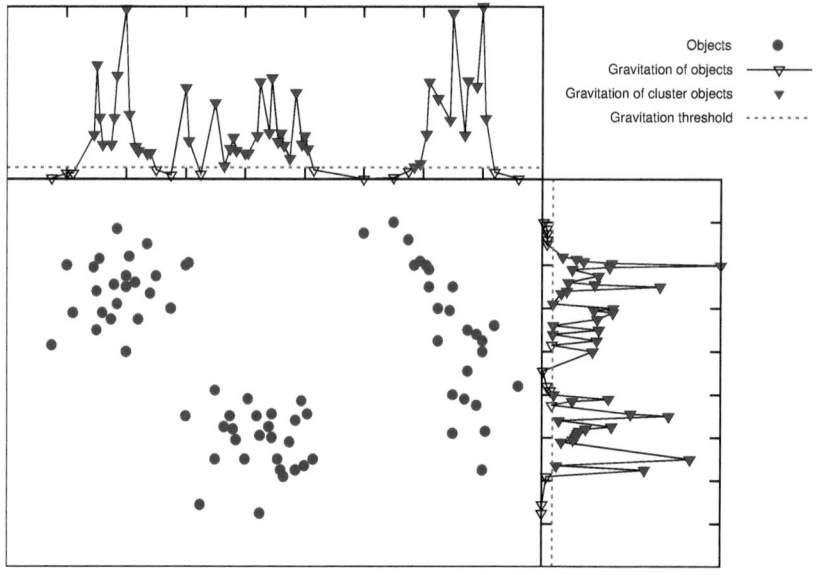

Figure 3.5: An example of SUGRA in two-dimensional data set

The detailed algorithm is shown in algorithm 2.

Reduction of redundancy

The final step is to reduce the small subspace clusters, and to keep only the largest subspace clusters. Because a big subspace cluster contains already the necessary information of a small one.

If $S > S'$, S' will be removed and only S will be retained in the final clustering results.

3.3 Automatic Subspace Clustering with the Distance-Density Function (ASCDD)

3.3.1 Motivation of ASCDD

In section 3.2, we have introduced the SUGRA (Subspace Clustering with the Gravitation Function) [Zhao 10a], which applies the gravitation function for calculating the density distribution in each single subspace and locates the high-dimensional subspace clusters with the bottom-up principle. SUGRA works well in many situations. However, the bottom-up methods have a common problem that it is difficult to explore clusters with concave forms in a high-dimensional subspace.

In order to discover high-dimensional subspace clusters with any forms and to minimize the number of parameters, we developed SUGRA into another subspace clustering algorithm with the name ASCDD (Automatic Subspace Clustering with the Distance-Density Function). ASCDD's density function is modified from the gravitation function of SUGRA and can be applied directly to any subspace. Moreover, ASCDD applies entropy to locate possible subspaces with clusters, and adapts the idea of neighborhood expansion to find clusters with any forms.

The following items are our concrete requirements for ASCDD:

- The density function should be applicable directly to objects in any high-dimensional subspace. The density values should have significant differences between cluster objects and non-cluster objects.

- Applying entropy to detect potential subspaces with clusters.

3. SUBSPACE CLUSTERING METHODS

- The clustering method should find subspace clusters with any forms, especially concave forms.

- The scale of density values should not depend on the types or scales of the objects, e.g. the density values of "salary" and "age" should have the same range.

3.3.2 Distance-Density function

An important definition of ASCDD is distance-density function, which measures the density value of two objects. The distance-density function of ASCDD is developed from SUGRA's density function for the purpose of directly calculating the density values of objects in any subspace.

Definition 3.12. *The distance-density of objects o_i and o_j with regard to subspace $\tilde{A}$ is defined as follows:*

$$d^{\tilde{A}}_{o_i,o_j} = \frac{1}{\left(\left(r^{\tilde{A}}_{o_i,o_j}\right)^2 \cdot |\mathcal{O}| + 1\right)^2} \tag{3.19}$$

where $r^{\tilde{A}}_{o_i,o_j} \in [0,1]$ is the normalized Euclidean distance defined in equation 3.6. $|\mathcal{O}|$ is the number of objects and has a value $\gg 1$. The distance-density $d^{\tilde{A}}_{o_i,o_j}$ has then a value ≤ 1.

From the distance-density of two objects, we define the density function of a single object in the subspace $\tilde{A}$ as follows:

Definition 3.13. *Distance-density of a single object o_i with regard to $\tilde{A}$ is the sum of the distance-density of the object o_i to all other objects in the subspace*

3.3 ASCDD

$\widetilde{\mathcal{A}}$:

$$D_{o_i}^{\widetilde{\mathcal{A}}} = \sum_{\forall o_j} d_{o_i,o_j}^{\widetilde{\mathcal{A}}} = \sum_{\forall o_j} \frac{1}{\left(\left(r_{o_i,o_j}^{\widetilde{\mathcal{A}}}\right)^2 \cdot |\mathcal{O}| + 1\right)^2} \quad (3.20)$$

$D_{o_i}^{\widetilde{\mathcal{A}}}$ has the value > 0. However, the maximal density value depends on the number of objects. Generally, the larger the number of objects is, the higher is the maximal density.

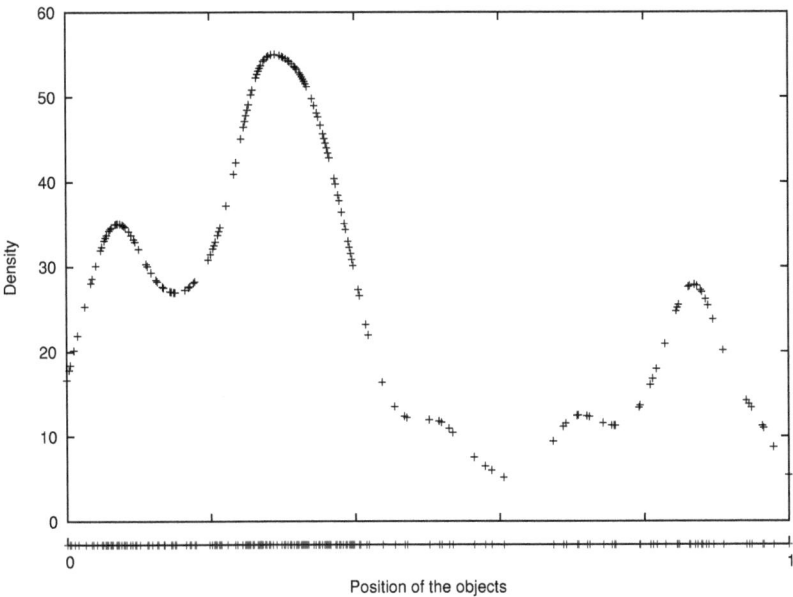

Figure 3.6: An example of the distance-density function of ASCDD

Figure 3.6 and figure 3.7 show examples of one-dimensional and two-dimensional objects with their distance-densities respectively. Similar to the gravitation function of SUGRA, the distance-density function of ASCDD can be consid-

3. SUBSPACE CLUSTERING METHODS

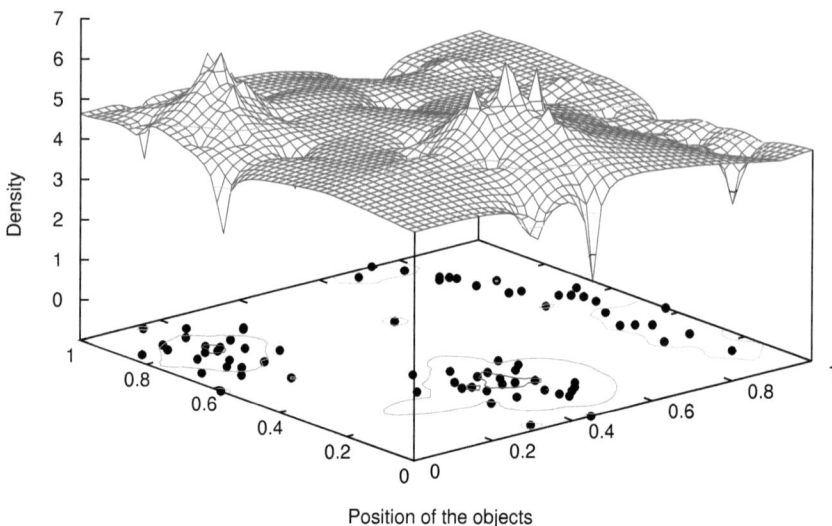

Figure 3.7: An example of the distance-density for a two-dimensional subspace with AS-CDD

ered as a distribution function that indicates the positions of dense and sparse objects. Comparing the differences of densities between cluster objects and non-cluster objects is an essential part of the clustering process. High peaks indicate dense objects, which are possible centers of clusters; Conversely, valleys point out sparse objects, which are usually boundaries of clusters or non-cluster objects.

The density of a single object is influenced more by its local surrounding objects than the objects beyond. For example, the density of an object will be higher if a new object is inserted nearby, but the densities of objects far from it will not change much.

As shown in figure 3.8, the evenly distributed objects do not have the same

3.3 ASCDD

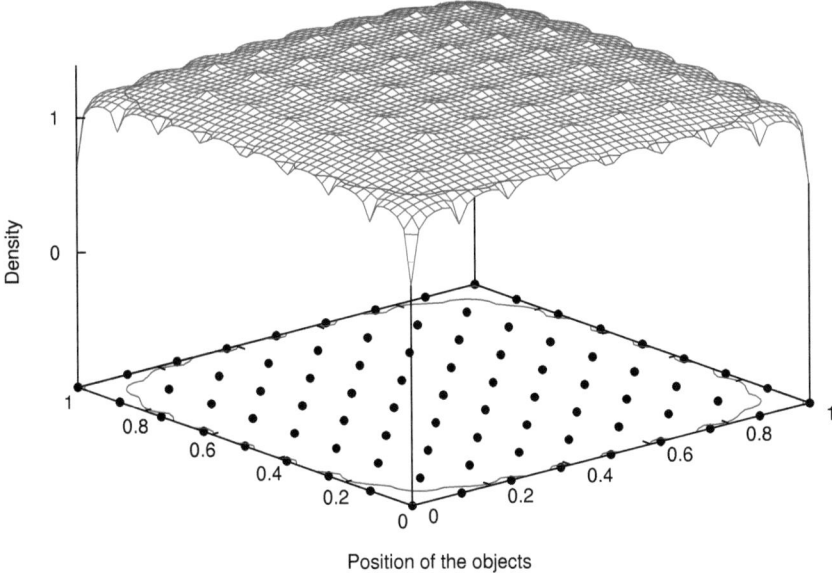

Figure 3.8: An example of distance-density of evenly distributed objects with ASCDD

density value, because the densities of objects in the middle are a little bigger than the densities at the edge. Nevertheless, the densities between objects in the center and at the edge are not very different compared to situations where clusters clearly exist.

Compared with SUGRA's density function that can be applied only to a one-dimensional subspace, the distance-density function of ASCDD is applicable not only in a one-dimensional subspace but in any subspace, because ASCDD does not have to sort the objects, which is especially convenient in high-dimensional subspaces. Generally speaking, ASCDD is more efficient than SUGRA for high-dimensional subspaces. However, unlike SUGRA, which can separate clusters with a single constant threshold $\overline{G^a}$, ASCDD does not have such properties, because the range of density values in ASCDD changes with the number of objects. Another small improvement of ASCDD compared to SUGRA is the treatment for the situation if $r^{\tilde{A}}_{o_i,o_j} = 0$, the distance-density of ASCDD is then $d^{\tilde{A}}_{o_i,o_j} = \frac{1}{(0+1)^2} = 1$, whereas SUGRA can not calculate the density directly and has to handle this case specially.

3.3.3 Find potential subspaces with entropy

Although ASCDD can be directly applied in any subspace, it is impractical to search clusters in all subspaces. Which subspaces have possibly clusters? We utilize entropy for detecting the potential subspaces. The authors of ENCLUS [Chen 99] introduced a method of applying entropy for detecting subspaces, which inspired us to apply entropy in ASCDD. However, ASCDD calculates and applies entropy for subspace detection in a different way.

Definition 3.14. *The Shannon entropy [Shan 48] for a discrete random variable X with n possible outcomes $\{x_i : i = 1, \cdots, n\}$ is defined as follows:*

$$H(X) = -\sum_{\forall i=1}^{n} p(x_i) \log p(x_i) \qquad (3.21)$$

where $p(\cdot)$ is the probability mass function.

Entropy plays a role in information theory as a measure of the amount of uncertainty with regard to a random variable. An important property of the entropy is that the variables with more uncertainty have lower entropy than the variables with less uncertainty. In the clustering tasks, we can say that a subspace with clusters has a lower entropy than a subspace without clusters.

3.3 ASCDD

The entropy $H(X)$ is larger than 0. The entropy reaches the maximum if all outcomes are equally probable, when $\forall i : p(x_i) = \frac{1}{n}$. The maximal entropy has the value $\log n$ that is calculated as follows:

$$H(X) \leq H(\frac{1}{n}, \cdots, \frac{1}{n}) = -\sum_{i=1}^{n} \frac{1}{n} \log \frac{1}{n} = \log n \quad (3.22)$$

As we described above, $H(X)$ lies in the range $[0, \log n]$. However, if $H(X)$ does not depend on n it is much more convenient for the comparison between data sets with different number of objects. For this purpose, we use the normalized entropy $E(X)$, which is defined as follows:

Definition 3.15 (Normalized entropy).

$$E(X) = \frac{H(X)}{\log n} = -\sum_{\forall i=1}^{n} p(x_i) \frac{\log p(x_i)}{\log n} \quad (3.23)$$

The normalized entropy $E(X)$ has the range $[0, 1]$, and does not depend on n. Similar to $H(X)$, $E(X)$ has also the same property of measuring the uncertainties.

Unlike ENCLUS, the probability of an object o_i on a subspace $\widetilde{A}$ is defined as the proportion of its density value to the sum of density values of entire objects, which is described as follows:

Definition 3.16 (Probability of an object).

$$p(o_i) = \frac{D_{o_i}^{\widetilde{A}}}{\sum_{\forall i} D_{o_i}^{\widetilde{A}}} \quad (3.24)$$

Obviously $p(o_i) \in [0, 1]$, $\sum_{\forall i} p(o_i) = 1$ and an object o_i with high density has also a large value $p(o_i)$. Therefore, the definition corresponds to the probability mass function.

As mentioned above, we apply the normalized entropy in ASCDD in order to facilitate calculating and comparing entropy values for any subspace. The entropy mentioned in the remaining part of this dissertation refers to the normalized entropy, which can be seen in the following definition.

Definition 3.17. $E(\widetilde{\mathcal{A}})$ is the normalized entropy with regard to a subspace $\widetilde{\mathcal{A}}$.

$$E(\widetilde{\mathcal{A}}) = -\sum_{\forall i=1}^{n} p(o_i) \frac{\log p(o_i)}{\log n} \tag{3.25}$$

Since $p(o_i)$ is calculable in any subspace, the entropy $E(\widetilde{\mathcal{A}})$ is then also applicable in any subspace. Moreover, because the value of $E(\widetilde{\mathcal{A}})$ depends on the densities of objects in $\widetilde{\mathcal{A}}$, $E(\widetilde{\mathcal{A}})$ reflects the distribution of objects in this subspace. A small $E(\widetilde{\mathcal{A}})$ indicates more uncertainties in $\widetilde{\mathcal{A}}$, which means there is a big chance to detect clusters in $\widetilde{\mathcal{A}}$. Contrarily, a big $E(\widetilde{\mathcal{A}})$ shows that the objects are distributed more uniformly in $\widetilde{\mathcal{A}}$ than in the subspaces with small entropy.

The maximal value of $E(\widetilde{\mathcal{A}})$ should be 1. However, as described before, the evenly distributed objects have little difference in density between middle objects and objects at edges. Therefore, a subspace with evenly distributed objects has a value of $E(\widetilde{\mathcal{A}})$ very close to 1.

Since it is impractical to traverse all possible $2^{|\mathcal{A}|}$ subspaces, our aim is to find the subspaces with possible clusters. We call a subspace with possible clusters a "potential subspace".

Comparing the entropy of different subspaces can help us to detect potential subspaces. A subspace $\widetilde{\mathcal{A}}$ and a higher-dimensional subspace $\widetilde{\mathcal{A}} \cup \widetilde{\mathcal{A}}'$ (with $\widetilde{\mathcal{A}} \cap \widetilde{\mathcal{A}}' = \emptyset$) have the following properties:

- If $E(\widetilde{\mathcal{A}} \cup \widetilde{\mathcal{A}}') < E(\widetilde{\mathcal{A}})$, then the subspace $\widetilde{\mathcal{A}} \cup \widetilde{\mathcal{A}}'$ has more clearly separated clusters than $\widetilde{\mathcal{A}}$.

3.3 ASCDD

- If $E(\widetilde{\mathcal{A}} \cup \widetilde{\mathcal{A}}') > E(\widetilde{\mathcal{A}})$, it is likely that $\widetilde{\mathcal{A}} \cup \widetilde{\mathcal{A}}'$ has more evenly distributed objects than $\widetilde{\mathcal{A}}$.

Suppose $\widetilde{\mathcal{A}}$ is a potential subspace. We use the following principle to check whether a higher-dimensional subspace $\widetilde{\mathcal{A}} \cup \{a_i\}$ is also a potential subspace:

$$E(\widetilde{\mathcal{A}} \cup \{a_i\}) \leq \min(\{E(X) \,|\, \forall X \subset \widetilde{\mathcal{A}} \cup \{a_i\}\}) \qquad (3.26)$$

If $E(\widetilde{\mathcal{A}} \cup \{a_i\})$ is not bigger than the entropy of any subspace of $\widetilde{\mathcal{A}} \cup \{a_i\}$, then subspace a_i can be integrated into subspace $\widetilde{\mathcal{A}}$, and $\widetilde{\mathcal{A}} \cup \{a_i\}$ is also a potential subspace. For instance, suppose that the current subspace is $\widetilde{\mathcal{A}} = \{a_1\}$, if $E(a_1, a_2) < \min(E(a_1), E(a_2))$ then $\widetilde{\mathcal{A}}$ will be expanded to $\widetilde{\mathcal{A}} = \{a_1, a_2\}$.

In order to maximize the dimensionality of each potential subspace, the maximal dimensionality is defined as follows:

Definition 3.18 (Maximal dimensionality of a potential subspace). *A potential subspace $\widetilde{\mathcal{A}}$ reaches its maximal dimensionality, if $\widetilde{\mathcal{A}}$ satisfies the condition:*

$$\forall a_i : \; E(\widetilde{\mathcal{A}}) < E(\widetilde{\mathcal{A}} \cup \{a_i\}) \qquad (3.27)$$

If a potential subspace $\widetilde{\mathcal{A}}$ reaches its maximal dimensionality, $\widetilde{\mathcal{A}}$ has more uncertainty than any of its supersets. So $\widetilde{\mathcal{A}}$ will be taken for searching clusters as the final subspace and its superset will not be considered.

The process of searching for potential subspaces starts from the one-dimensional subspace with the lowest entropy. The current subspace is then expanded to its maximal dimensionality. After that, we search the next one-dimensional subspace with the lowest entropy from the remaining subspaces and repeat the process. The process stops when all subspaces have reached the maximal dimensionality.

3. SUBSPACE CLUSTERING METHODS

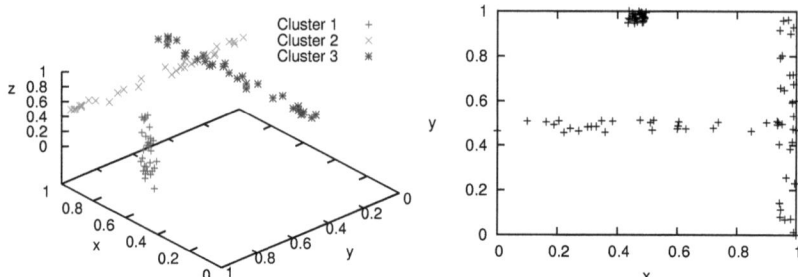

Figure 3.9: An example of detecting a potential subspace

Figure 3.9 shows an example of how to detect potential subspaces. In this example there are obviously three clusters. However, it is not straightforward to find them directly in the three-dimensional space $\{x, y, z\}$, but if the objects are projected into each two-dimensional subspace, the clustering process will be more effective. In each two-dimensional subspace, one cluster is much tighter than the other two clusters, namely, the two-dimensional subspaces $\{x, y\}$, $\{y, z\}$, $\{x, z\}$ have more distinct cluster distribution than the three-dimensional space. As illustrated in figure 3.10, when the objects are projected into the subspace $\{x, y\}$, the density distribution of objects is much clearer than that in $\{x, y, z\}$. Similarly, subspaces $\{x, z\}$ and $\{y, z\}$ have also clearer density distribution than $\{x, y, z\}$.

The above result can also be verified through the principle of detecting subspaces. The calculation of the entropy shows that the subspaces have the following relations:

$$E(x,y); E(y,z); E(x,z) < E(x); E(y); E(z) < E(x,y,z) \qquad (3.28)$$

Equation 3.28 indicates that the entropy of a two-dimensional subspace is smaller than the entropy of a one-dimensional and a three-dimensional subspace. Thus

3.3 ASCDD

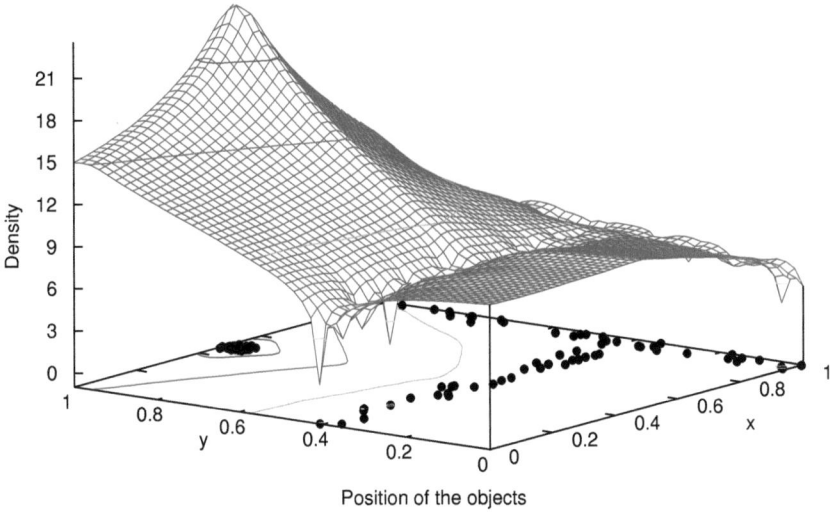

Figure 3.10: Distance-density of objects in the subspace {x,y}

each two-dimensional subspace reaches the maximal dimensionality.

The details of the subspace searching process of the example figure 3.9 are shown as follows:

1. ASCDD searches firstly a one-dimensional subspace $\{x\}$. Then it checks $\{x,y\}$: Since $E(x,y) < E(x)$, $\{x\}$ is expanded to $\{x,y\}$.

2. In the next step, it checks $\{x,y,z\}$: Because $E(x,y) < E(x,y,z)$, $\{x,y\}$ will not expand to $\{x,y,z\}$, which means that $\{x,y\}$ has the maximal dimensionality.

3. The next potential subspace is $\{y\}$. Since $\{x,y\}$ is already checked, we check then $\{y,z\}$. Like $\{x,y\}$, the subspace $\{y,z\}$ is the next potential subspace with maximal dimensionality.

4. Similarly, we find the last potential subspace $\{z,x\}$ with maximal dimensionality from $\{z\}$.

As described above, the search for potential subspaces stops at each two-dimensional subspace $\{x,y\}$, $\{y,z\}$ and $\{z,x\}$, whereas the three-dimensional space is not considered because the two-dimensional subspaces reach the maximal dimensionality.

3.3.4 Exploring clusters

The positions and densities of clusters are indicated by the distance-density function. The objects with high densities are possible cluster objects, meanwhile objects at the edges of clusters have lower densities. The density of an object is mainly determined by the other objects in its local environment, so a cluster could consist of an object with high density and its neighbors. The main purpose of this section is to establish a way of assigning objects and their surrounding objects to the corresponding clusters.

One question is how to find clusters from the objects with large distance-density values. Since neighboring objects with high density values belong possibly to the same cluster, we search the neighboring objects from high density to low density.

The main idea of searching clusters in a subspace consists of the following two main steps:

1. Searching for the neighbors of an object with the highest density

2. Maximizing clusters by extending neighborhoods

The objects of a cluster consist of directly connected neighbors and the expansion of neighbors. Figure 3.11 shows an example of two clusters that are

3.3 ASCDD

labeled with different colors. As illustrated in the figure, the objects are surrounded by circles. The circle indicates the neighborhood of its corresponding central object, which means the objects within the same circle are considered as neighbors. The determination of the radius will be introduced later.

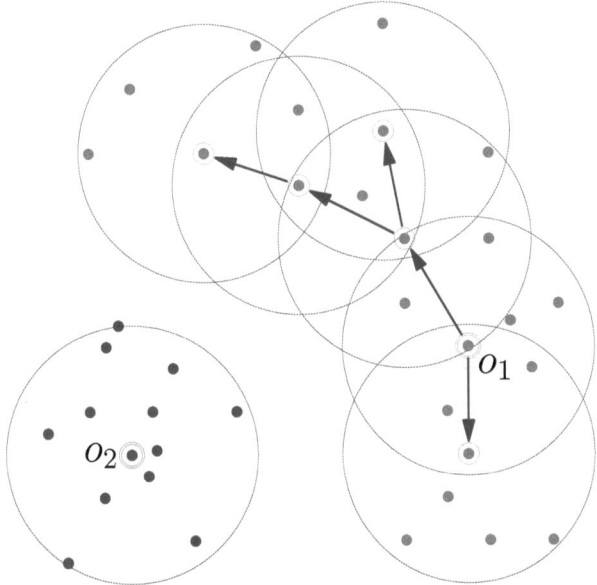

Figure 3.11: Neighboring objects

If a central object of a circle belongs to another circle, then the two circles are "connected". All objects in a cluster are connected through the circles. Meanwhile, the objects from different clusters can not be connected through any circle.

In this example, the clustering process starts from a start object o_1, who has the maximal density. As a central object, o_1 has neighbors in its circle. Each new neighboring object can have also further neighbors. For example, the figure illustrates two new circles towards two directions. From the new circles, we can find further neighbors. All the objects in the connected circles form a cluster. The other cluster consists of only the objects in the circle of the central object o_2 and it can not be expanded with further new neighbors from the objects in this cluster. The objects in the first cluster are not connected with the objects in the second cluster through the neighbor-expansion.

This process is similar to but not the same as DBSCAN [Este 96]. The main differences are:

- The determination of the start object is different. DBSCAN finds a start object, whose neighborhood has the number of objects larger than $MinPts$, whereas ASCDD takes the object with the highest density as the start object, which does not require any parameters.

- DBSCAN defines neighborhood based on Euclidean distance. The distance of two directly density-connected objects should smaller than the parameter ε, which should be determined differently on diverse subspaces. ASCDD determines the neighborhood based on their density differences, whose range does not depend on the subspaces.

As we mentioned above, an important procedure in ASCDD is to determine the size of circles and to check whether two objects are neighbors. The details will be introduced in the next two paragraphs.

Searching neighbors of an object

3.3 ASCDD

Definition 3.19 (The set of neighbors). *The set of neighbors of an object o_i in subspace $\widetilde{A}$ is defined as follows:*

$$Neighbor(o_i^{\widetilde{A}}) = \{o_j | \, d_{o_i,o_j}^{\widetilde{A}} > DDT\} \tag{3.29}$$

where DDT(Distance-Density Threshold) is a threshold for choosing neighbors.

From the above definition, only the objects with distance-density to the center object $o_i^{\widetilde{A}}$ higher than DDT meet the condition and will be considered as neighbors of $o_i^{\widetilde{A}}$.

The DDT value is equivalent to the radius of circles, which can affect the number of neighbors or the size of clusters. Generally, the larger DDT is chosen, the fewer neighbors are selected. So choosing a proper DDT is important. Since $d_{o_i,o_j}^{\widetilde{A}}$ has a value between 0 and 1, the parameter DDT has also to be determined within the range $(0,1)$. However, a too small or too big value of DDT can cause that the whole objects belong to one cluster or there is no cluster. So a proper value for DDT should be set in $(0,1)$. However, it is still problematic to pick a value for DDT in $(0,1)$, so the range for choosing DDT must be smaller.

We notice that these two values are important for the determination of DDT.

$$T_{min}^{\widetilde{A}} = \min_{\forall i} \left(\max_{\forall j \neq i} (d_{o_i,o_j}^{\widetilde{A}}) \right) \tag{3.30}$$

and

$$T_{max}^{\widetilde{A}} = \max_{\forall i} \left(\max_{\forall j \neq i} (d_{o_i,o_j}^{\widetilde{A}}) \right) \tag{3.31}$$

where $\max_{\forall j \neq i}(d_{o_i,o_j}^{\widetilde{A}})$ is the maximal distance-density of o_i with regard to the subspace $\widetilde{A}$. Obviously, if o_j has the minimal Euclidean distance to o_i then o_i has

3. SUBSPACE CLUSTERING METHODS

the maximal distance-density value with o_j in $\widetilde{\mathcal{A}}$. $T_{min}^{\widetilde{\mathcal{A}}}$ and $T_{max}^{\widetilde{\mathcal{A}}}$ are the smallest and biggest maximal distance-density of all objects with regard to $\widetilde{\mathcal{A}}$. Notice that $T_{min}^{\widetilde{\mathcal{A}}}$ and $T_{max}^{\widetilde{\mathcal{A}}}$ are different according to diverse $\widetilde{\mathcal{A}}$.

These two values affect the clustering results as follows:

- If $DDT \geq T_{max}^{\widetilde{\mathcal{A}}}$, no object is assigned to any cluster, because no object has a neighbor.

- If $DDT < T_{min}^{\widetilde{\mathcal{A}}}$, all objects are selected as one cluster, because all objects are connected through the neighborhood.

Obviously, DDT should be set between $T_{min}^{\widetilde{\mathcal{A}}}$ and $T_{max}^{\widetilde{\mathcal{A}}}$ to obtain a clustering result, therefore we can define DDT as follows:

Definition 3.20 (Definition of DDT).

$$DDT = q \cdot T_{min}^{\widetilde{\mathcal{A}}} + (1-q) \cdot T_{max}^{\widetilde{\mathcal{A}}}, \ 0 < q < 1 \tag{3.32}$$

Figure 3.12 illustrates an example of values $T_{min}^{\widetilde{\mathcal{A}}}$ and $T_{max}^{\widetilde{\mathcal{A}}}$. o_{min} and o_{max} are the objects with the distance-density value $T_{min}^{\widetilde{\mathcal{A}}}$ and $T_{max}^{\widetilde{\mathcal{A}}}$ respectively. If DDT is close to $T_{min}^{\widetilde{\mathcal{A}}}$, many objects with distance-density values bigger than $T_{min}^{\widetilde{\mathcal{A}}}$ have the chances to be selected in the next step. Conversely, if DDT is close to $T_{max}^{\widetilde{\mathcal{A}}}$, the number of selected objects will be much smaller. So by setting DDT close to $T_{min}^{\widetilde{\mathcal{A}}}$ (when q is close to 1), the clustering results become relative acceptable in most cases. The comparison of clustering results by choosing different q is illustrated in section 4.2.1.

Maximize clusters by extending neighborhoods

For exploring a cluster, ASCDD begins with searching neighbors of an object with the highest density, which is called the "start" object. Suppose

3.3 ASCDD

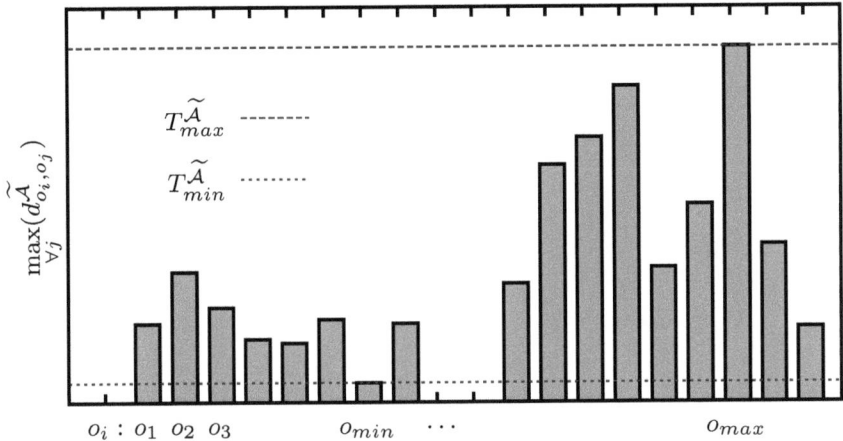

Figure 3.12: An example of $T_{min}^{\widetilde{A}}$ and $T_{max}^{\widetilde{A}}$

$o^{\widetilde{A}}$ is a start object. Its neighboring objects are firstly put into an initial set $\widetilde{O} = Neighbor(o^{\widetilde{A}})$. The next step is the expansion of $\widetilde{O}$, $\forall o_i^{\widetilde{A}} \in \widetilde{O}/\{o^{\widetilde{A}}\}$:

$$\text{if } Neighbor(o_i^{\widetilde{A}}) \neq \emptyset, \text{ then } \widetilde{O} = \widetilde{O} \cup Neighbor(o_i^{\widetilde{A}}) \qquad (3.33)$$

The new objects in $Neighbor(o_i^{\widetilde{A}})$ are added to the $\widetilde{O}$. This step is repeated for each new found object until no further new neighbors are found. Finally, $(\widetilde{A}, \widetilde{O})$ generates a cluster with the "start" object $o_i^{\widetilde{A}}$.

We have described above the way of exploring a cluster from a "start" object. However, how do we obtain the "start" objects from all objects? As shown in figure 3.6, the peaks with high density values reveal the positions of clusters. ASCDD firstly finds an object with the maximal density from the whole objects as the "start" object and then searches the objects related to the "start" object. Afterwards it finds the next object with the maximal density value from the rest of objects, namely the next "start" object.

3. SUBSPACE CLUSTERING METHODS

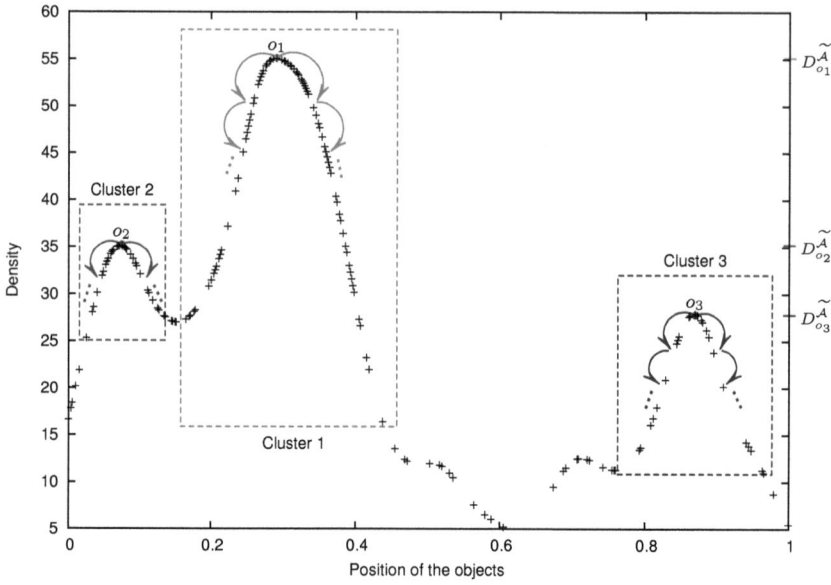

Figure 3.13: An example of clustering process of ASCDD

Figure 3.13 shows an example of a one-dimensional clustering process. In this example, the clustering process starts from the neighbors of object o_1 that has maximal density. Then it extends the objects in $Neighbor(o_1)$ until no more new objects are found. Cluster 1 is derived from o_1 and consists of objects from the extension of neighborhood. After we get cluster 1, the objects in cluster 1 are excluded and the next "start" object with the highest density in the rest of objects is o_2. The clustering process for cluster 2 is the same as cluster 1. Then we find cluster 3 from o_3, and so on. The clusters are explored in turn according to the densities of their "start" objects.

3.3 ASCDD

3.3.5 Algorithm of ASCDD

The clustering process of ASCDD consists of the following steps.

1. Search for potential subspaces

2. Exploration of clusters within the potential subspaces

3. Reduction of redundancy

Search for potential subspaces

As we discussed in section 3.3.3, the search for the potential subspaces is based on the entropy values. Algorithm 3 shows the process of the search for potential subspaces with the following steps:

1. We calculate the entropy of each one-dimensional subspace $E(a)$, $\forall a \in \mathcal{A}$.

2. Suppose a is a one-dimensional subspace with the lowest entropy, we expand a to the maximal dimensionality.

3. Then we search for the next one-dimensional subspace with the lowest entropy. Repeat step 2 until no more new one-dimensional subspaces exist.

Exploration of clusters within the potential subspaces

Algorithm 4 illustrates the process of the exploration of clusters in ASCDD. This process for a potential subspace $\widetilde{\mathcal{A}}$ is divided into four steps.

1. $\forall i$, the density value of each object $D_{o_i}^{\widetilde{\mathcal{A}}}$ is calculated.

Algorithm 3: Search for potential subspaces in ASCDD

Input: $(\mathcal{A}, \mathcal{O})$

Output: Potential subspace set: PSS

1 calculating entropy of each subspace $E(a_i), \forall a_i \in \mathcal{A}$
2 ascending sort $E(a_i)$
3 $PSS = \emptyset$
4 **for** $i = 1$ *to* $|\mathcal{A}|$ **do**
5 $\quad \mathcal{C} = \{a_i\}$
6 $\quad$ **for** $j = i+1$ *to* $|\mathcal{A}|$ **do**
7 $\quad\quad minEntropy = \min(E(\mathcal{C}), E(a_j))$
8 $\quad\quad$ **if** $E(\mathcal{C} \cup \{a_j\})$ <*minEntropy* **then**
9 $\quad\quad\quad \mathcal{C} = \mathcal{C} \cup \{a_j\}$
10 $\quad\quad$ **end**
11 $\quad$ **end**
12 $\quad PSS = PSS \cup \{\mathcal{C}\}$
13 **end**
14 **return** PSS

2. We find the "start" object o_s with the maximal density from the current set of objects $O_{current}$.

3. Then we insert all neighbors of o_s and the connected neighbors into S.

4. The objects of S are then removed from $O_{current}$, repeat step 2 until no more new clusters are found.

3.3 ASCDD

Algorithm 4: Exploration of clusters in ASCDD

Input: $(\mathcal{A}, \mathcal{O})$, Potential subspace set: PSS

Output: Set of all clusters $\hat{S}$

1   $\hat{S} = \emptyset$
2   **foreach** $\widetilde{\mathcal{A}} \subseteq PSS$ **do**
3      $\mathcal{O}_{current} = \mathcal{O}$
4      $\forall i$, calculate $D_{o_i}^{\widetilde{\mathcal{A}}}$
5   **while** $\mathcal{O}_{current} \neq \emptyset$ **do**
6   o_s has max $(d_{o_i}^{\widetilde{\mathcal{A}}})$, $\forall o_i \in \mathcal{O}_{current}$
7         $\widetilde{O} = Neighbor(o_s)$
8   Iteration: $\forall o_i \in \widetilde{O}$, $Neighbor(o_i) \subseteq \widetilde{O}$
9         $\mathcal{O}_{current} = \mathcal{O}_{current} - \widetilde{O}$
10        $S = (\widetilde{\mathcal{A}}, \widetilde{O})$, $\hat{S} = \hat{S} \cup S$
11   **end**
12 **end**
13 **return** $\hat{S}$

Reduction of redundancy

Similar to SUGRA, we eliminate the small subspace clusters and keep only the large ones.

If the clustering results include two clusters S and S' with the relation $S > S'$, then S is kept in the clustering result, and S' is removed as a redundancy.

3.4 Summary

We introduced our subspace clustering methods SUGRA and ASCDD with their ideas, definitions, properties and algorithms in this chapter.

In the next chapter, we will discuss more details about these two methods and compare them with other subspace clustering algorithms.

4

DISCUSSION & COMPARISON

We have introduced two subspace clustering approaches SUGRA and AS-CDD in chapter 3. However, there are still many unexplained questions. In this chapter, we discuss more about these two algorithms and compare different subspace clustering methods.

4.1 Discussion about SUGRA

SUGRA (Subspace Clustering with the Gravitation Function) is introduced in section 3.2. It separates cluster objects by using a gravitation threshold. We will analyze the main advantages and disadvantages of this subspace clustering algorithm.

4.1.1 Parameter choice

In the algorithm SUGRA, the parameter gravitation threshold should approximate theoretically 3.29. We can use 3.29 as the gravitation threshold in many situations. However, this value could vary a little in some situations in order to find the "desired" clusters. This happens if the cluster boundary is not "clear", so that the gravitation threshold could be bigger or smaller than 3.29 to separate the vague clusters.

4. DISCUSSION & COMPARISON

The value 3.29 can be set as a starting point for choosing the gravitation threshold. Although a manual regulation near 3.29 may be sometimes necessary, it is still simpler to choose a parameter near 3.29 than to determine the parameters for other approaches, where the parameters have to be selected from unknown ranges.

4.1.2 Data scale

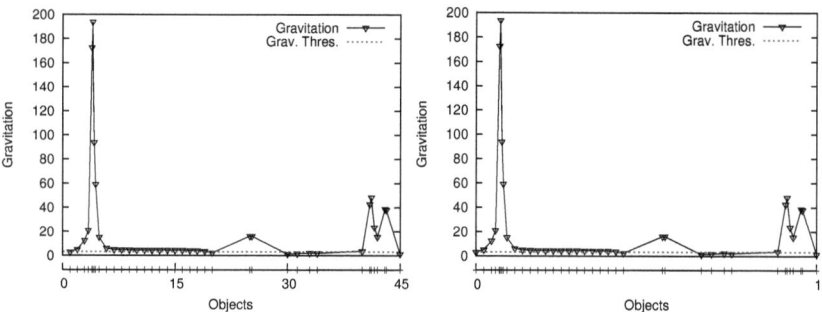

Figure 4.1: Gravitation values with different scales of data

SUGRA finds clusters based on the distribution of objects and does not depend on the scale of data. For instance, if the data are stretched proportional to another scale, the gravitation values will not change. As shown in figure 4.1, a data set has the same gravitation values before and after the normalization (see x-axis). With this property, the data with different scales could be compared simply.

4.1 DISCUSSION ABOUT SUGRA

4.1.3 Cluster shapes

The biggest limitation of SUGRA is that it is difficult to find clusters with concave forms in a high-dimensional subspace, especially if the concave clusters are interlaced. The mixed clusters are usually extracted together as one big cluster or separated to small ones.

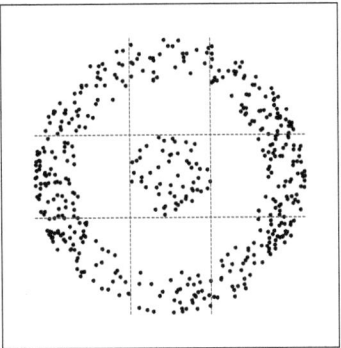

Figure 4.2: An example of concave clusters

An example in figure 4.2 shows that the objects in the middle area have much higher gravitation values than those at the side. After projecting the objects to each one-dimensional subspace, SUGRA extracts objects in the middle as a cluster, however the outer objects with the ring form have relative small gravitation values and are fragmented into small ones.

Although it is possible to merge the small clusters into one big cluster (similar to CLIQUE), the merging process requires much extra run time and the clustering results may lose accuracy in a high-dimensional subspace. To avoid the limitation, we could use ASCDD for high-dimensional subspaces.

4. DISCUSSION & COMPARISON

4.2 Discussion about ASCDD

We have introduced ASCDD (Automatic Subspace Clustering with the Distance -Density Function) in section 3.3. As an improvement of SUGRA, ASCDD has many distinguishing characteristics. This section discusses the details of this method.

4.2.1 Parameter choice

ASCDD requires no parameter for the density calculation and subspace selection, but it needs one parameter (DDT) for searching the neighbors. As defined in definition 3.20, DDT correlates with $T_{min}^{\widetilde{A}}$ and $T_{max}^{\widetilde{A}}$, where $DDT = q \cdot T_{min}^{\widetilde{A}} + (1-q) \cdot T_{max}^{\widetilde{A}}$, $0 < q < 1$. The value of q decides the clustering result. Generally, a large q generates large clusters and a small q yields clusters with small sizes.

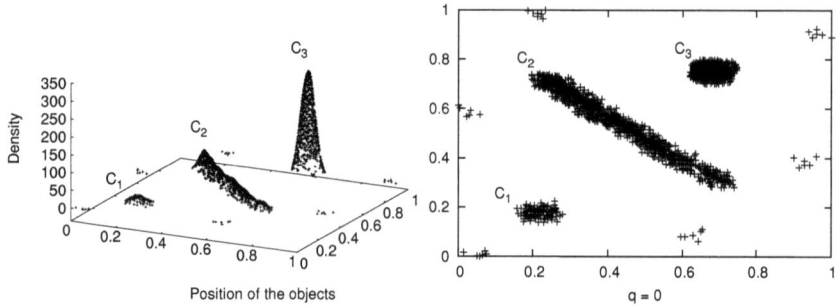

Figure 4.3: Density of objects and clustering result with $q = 0$

Figure 4.3 - figure 4.8 show the clustering results of a two-dimensional data set by setting q from 0 to 1. The cluster objects are presented with different

4.2 Discussion about ASCDD

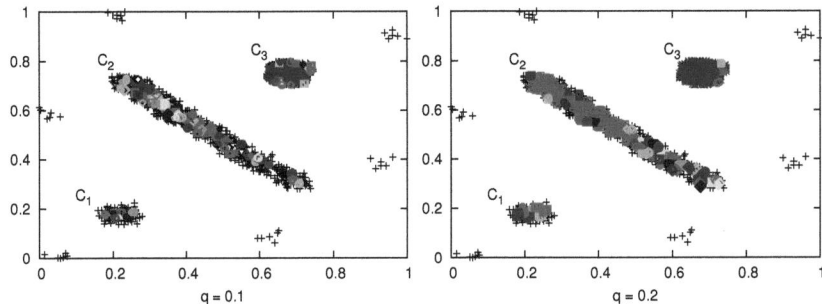

Figure 4.4: Clustering result with $q = 0.1$ and $q = 0.2$

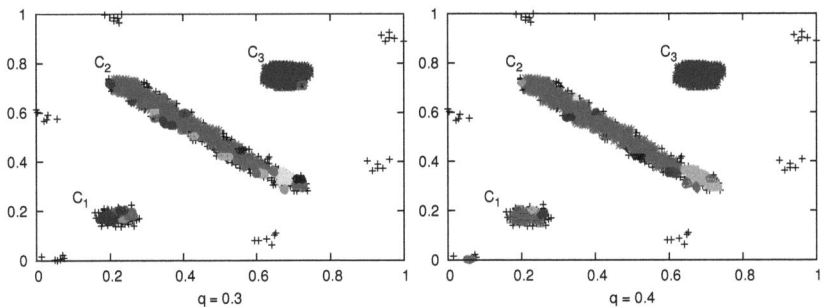

Figure 4.5: Clustering result with $q = 0.3$ and $q = 0.4$

colors. The first figure shows the density values of three clusters, where the cluster C_3 has much higher density than the clusters C_2 and C_1. For $q = 0$ there is no cluster extracted from the objects. By setting q close to 0, the clusters can be partitioned into small ones. As q increases to 1, the clustering results are getting stable.

Generally, a cluster with high density is less influenced by q than a cluster with low density. A cluster with low density can be easily split into smaller ones, especially when q has a small value. In this example C_1 and C_2 are separated

4. Discussion & Comparison

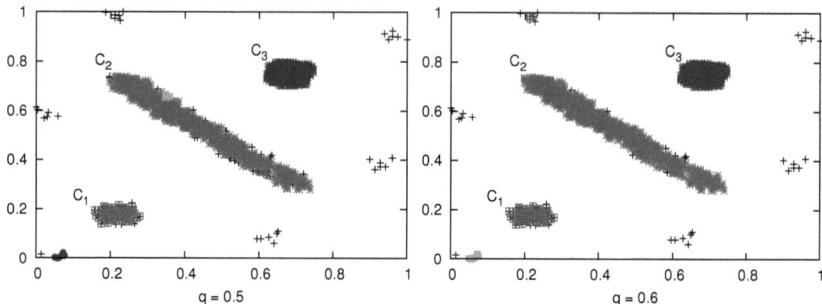

Figure 4.6: Clustering result with $q = 0.5$ and $q = 0.6$

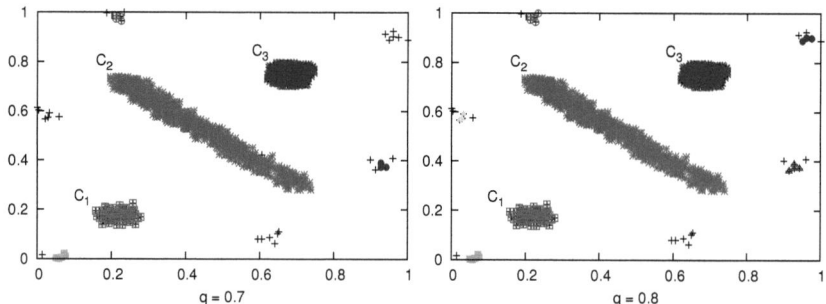

Figure 4.7: Clustering result with $q = 0.7$ and $q = 0.8$

into many small clusters when q is between 0.1 and 0.4. The figures show that C_3 has very similar clustering results when q is between 0.3 and 1, whereas C_1 and C_2 have similar results with q ranging from 0.5 to 1.

The comparison also shows that the clustering results are much better by setting a q close to 1. However, outliers can be included by clusters when q is set with a very large value. Contrarily, clusters include fewer objects when q is small. We suggest choosing a q close to 1. Nevertheless, according to the application, a fine tuning of q can yield a better clustering result.

4.2 DISCUSSION ABOUT ASCDD

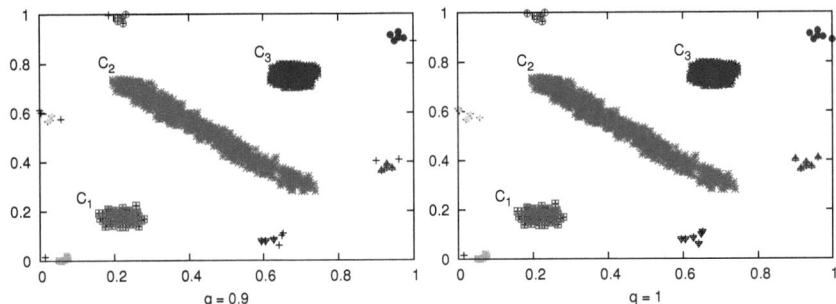

Figure 4.8: Clustering result with $q = 0.9$ and $q = 1$

4.2.2 Cluster shapes

It is not difficult to identify a convex shaped cluster with many clustering algorithms. However, not all the algorithms are able to find concave clusters. ASCDD could find arbitrary (convex and concave) shaped clusters.

As we discussed in section 3.3.4, the object with the highest density in a cluster is chosen as the "start" object. However, a "start" object is not necessarily the geometric center of a cluster. Figure 4.9 shows an example of two-dimensional clustered objects. Figure 4.10 illustrates the corresponding density values of the objects and clusters marked with different colors. The two clusters have both concave forms and the "start" objects o_1 and o_2 of the two clusters do not lie at their geometric centers but at the edges of the clusters, where the density is high. The cluster objects in the same cluster are all the extensions of neighborhoods from its "start" object. Through the addition of new neighbors, the objects in a cluster can be connected together to reach the concave shape of the cluster.

The clustering result of ASCDD does not depend on the input order of the objects, and furthermore it is not necessary to estimate the number of clusters.

4. DISCUSSION & COMPARISON

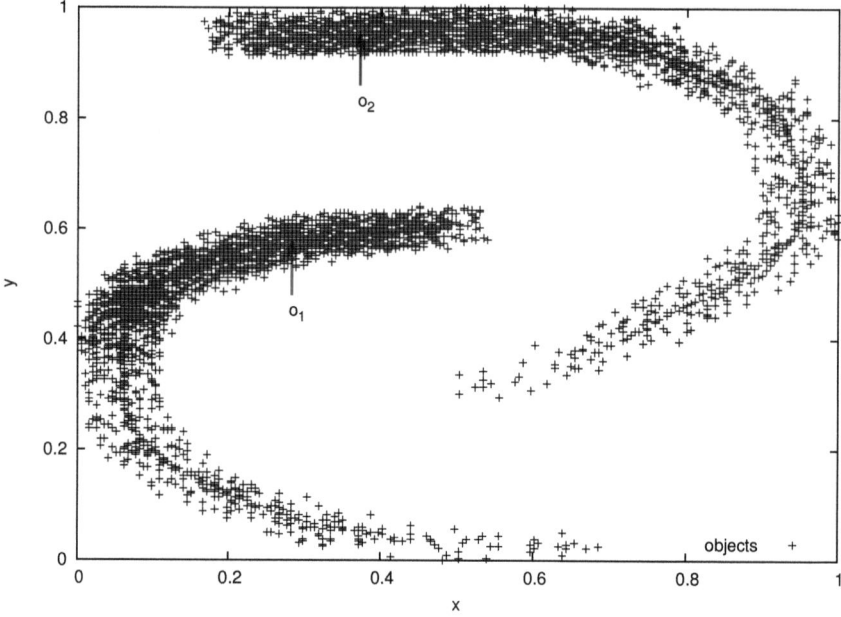

Figure 4.9: An example of two-dimensional concave clusters

This is due to the fact that the clusters are explored based on the density values of the "start" objects from the highest density to the lowest density, one by one.

ASCDD can solve the example shown in figure 4.2. The figure 4.11 illustrates the density values and clustering result with ASCDD. The objects in the middle circle area have much higher density than the objects in the ring. As a result, the two clusters can be clearly separated from each other.

4.2 DISCUSSION ABOUT ASCDD

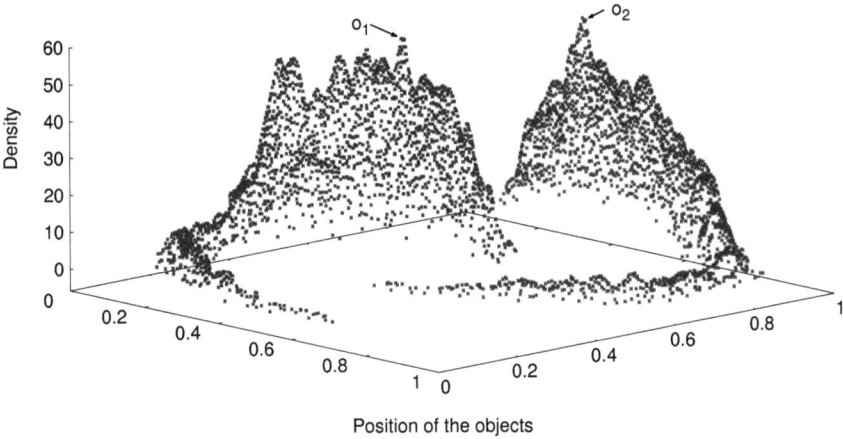

Figure 4.10: Density values of concave clusters

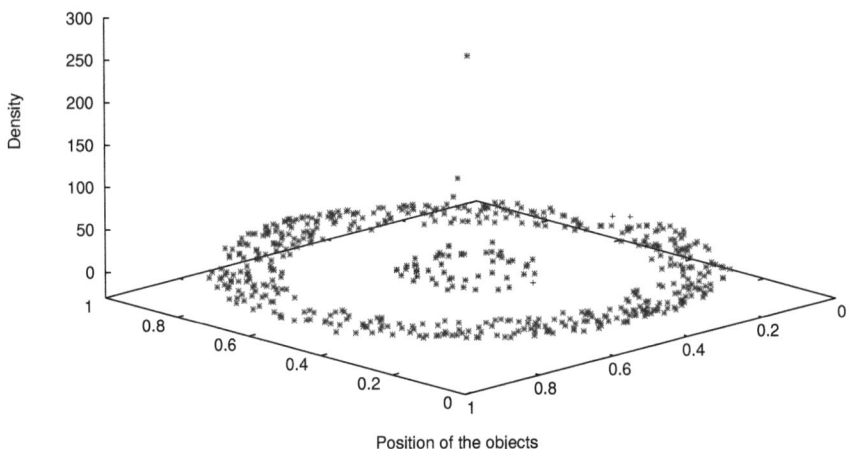

Figure 4.11: Clustering result with ASCDD

4.2.3 Time complexity

The time complexity of ASCDD depends on the number of objects $|\mathcal{O}|$ and dimensions $|\mathcal{A}|$ as well as on the number of potential subspace sets $|PSS|$. The run time of the density calculation is $O(|\mathcal{O}|^2)$ for one subspace. The number of possibly involved subspaces for density calculation can be from $|\mathcal{A}|$ to $2^{|\mathcal{A}|}$. The run time of searching subspaces depends on the cardinality of the potential subspace sets $|PSS|$, which has the range $(0, 2^{|\mathcal{A}|})$.

One idea for reducing the run time related to the number of objects is to apply sampling data. For example, by choosing $\frac{1}{n}$ entire objects as sampling objects, the run time is reduced to $\frac{1}{n^2}$. However, one problem is that the sampling data may be biased if they are not evenly selected, which may cause changing or even losing clusters.

4.3 Comparison

In this section, we compare some subspace clustering methods with respect to their algorithms and clustering results. It includes a comparison of SUGRA with ASCDD, as well as comparisons between these two methods and other subspace clustering methods with similar concepts.

4.3.1 SUGRA versus ASCDD

In SUGRA, the non-cluster objects have low density values in the range $[0, 3.29]$. Contrarily, the cluster objects have density values in the range > 3.29. However, the maximum gravitation can be very different, which does not depend on the number of objects but depends strongly on the local density. For example, if some objects are extremely close in comparison with other objects, the gravitation of these objects will be much higher than others. However, the non-cluster objects have still lower gravitation than the gravitation threshold. Generally, SUGRA is more sensitive to the local distance.

4.3 COMPARISON

Compared with SUGRA, ASCDD's density values are less sensitive to the local density. The difference of the maximum and minimum density is smaller than SUGRA. But ASCDD can not find a static threshold as SUGRA.

The figure 4.12 shows the clustering results on the same one-dimensional data set with SUGRA and ASCDD. Where SUGRA uses 3.29 as gravitation threshold, and ASCDD applies $q = 0.9$ as the parameter setting. SUGRA has a much "sharp" curve and ASCDD's curve is more "smooth". However, the clustering results with both methods are almost the same in this situation.

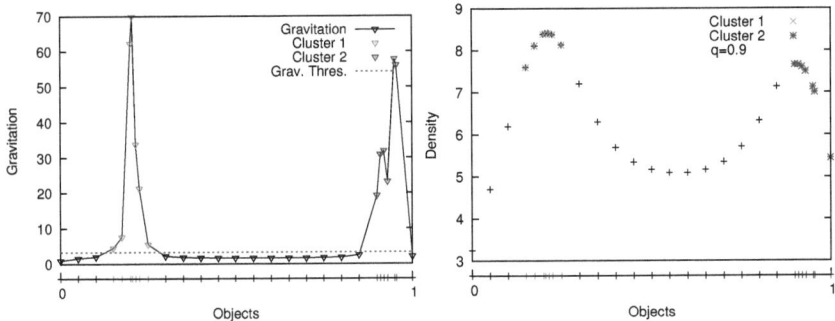

Figure 4.12: Comparison of clustering results with SUGRA and ASCDD

4.3.2 SUGRA versus CLIQUE

SUGRA and CLIQUE [Agra 98] are both bottom-up subspace clustering methods, which search clusters from low dimensional to high-dimensional subspaces. The two algorithms use very different approaches in searching for clusters. CLIQUE uses the process of "dividing objects", "searching high density areas", "merging the dense objects" to find clusters in one-dimensional subspaces. This manner of searching clusters can cause inaccuracy, because separating and

4. Discussion & Comparison

merging objects many times may lose cluster objects or yield big clusters. In comparison with CLIQUE, SUGRA takes one cut to separate the cluster and non-cluster objects, which yield the entire clusters at one time.

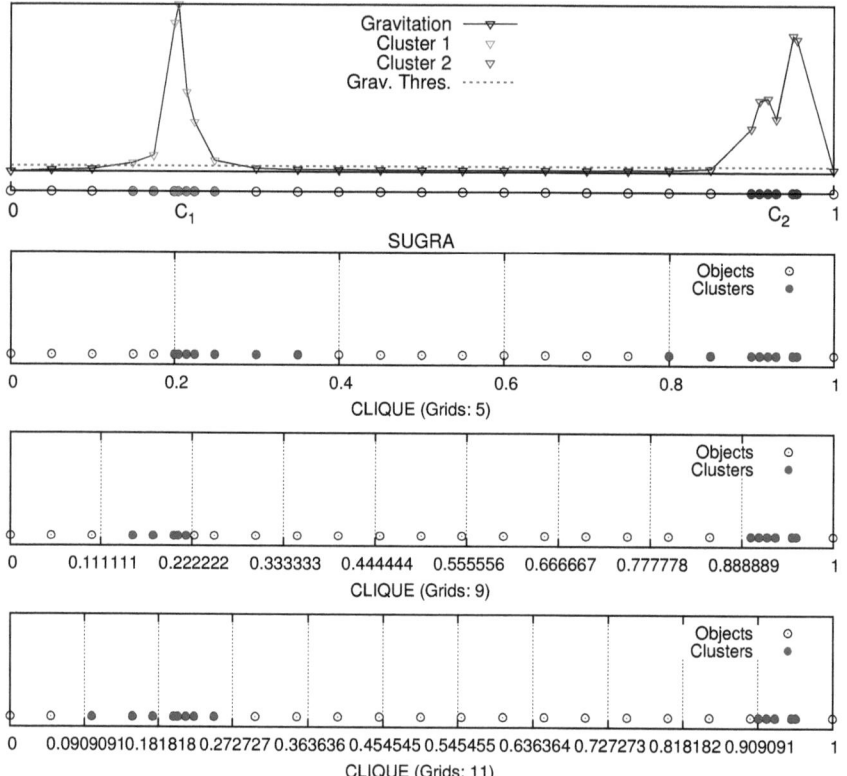

Figure 4.13: Comparison of clustering results with SUGRA and CLIQUE

The example in figure 4.13 shows the comparison of clustering results of SUGRA and CLIQUE on a one-dimensional subspace. SUGRA can find two clusters C_1 and C_2 simply, which are labeled with different colors. However,

4.3 COMPARISON

CLIQUE has very different results by choosing the different numbers of grids. For example, with 5 grids CLIQUE detects only a part of C_1, which is combined with some non-cluster objects together. Meanwhile, the cluster C_2 contains also some non-cluster objects. Choosing the number of grid cells with 9 or 11 produces similar situations, where the clusters are split or attached with non-cluster objects. The inaccuracy of CLIQUE is caused by the inexact dividing of objects by the grid, which is a common issue of grid-based subspace clustering algorithms. By contrast, SUGRA can locate the position of clusters more exactly.

4.3.3 ASCDD versus DENCLUE

Estimating the density values of objects by using density functions is a similarity between DENCLUE [Hinn 98] and ASCDD. DENCLUE applies the Gaussian kernel function (equation 2.1) and ASCDD uses the distance-density function (equation 3.19). The density values are calculated in different manners by applying these two functions.

Figure 4.14 shows the differences between the density functions of ASCDD and DENCLUE on a two-dimensional data set with three clusters. ASCDD determines directly the appropriate distribution of objects for the next clustering step, where the center of clusters have clearly higher density than other objects. However, DENCLUE has to choose the standard deviation σ as a parameter to estimate the distribution of objects. For example, by choosing the parameter $\sigma > 0.3$, there are no distinct clusters. By setting $\sigma \leq 0.2$, the distribution of objects allows to distinguish these clusters.

The above example indicates that choosing the parameters in DENCLUE plays a decisive role for estimating the densities and the clustering result. Whereas ASCDD does not need extra parameters to achieve the calculation of density.

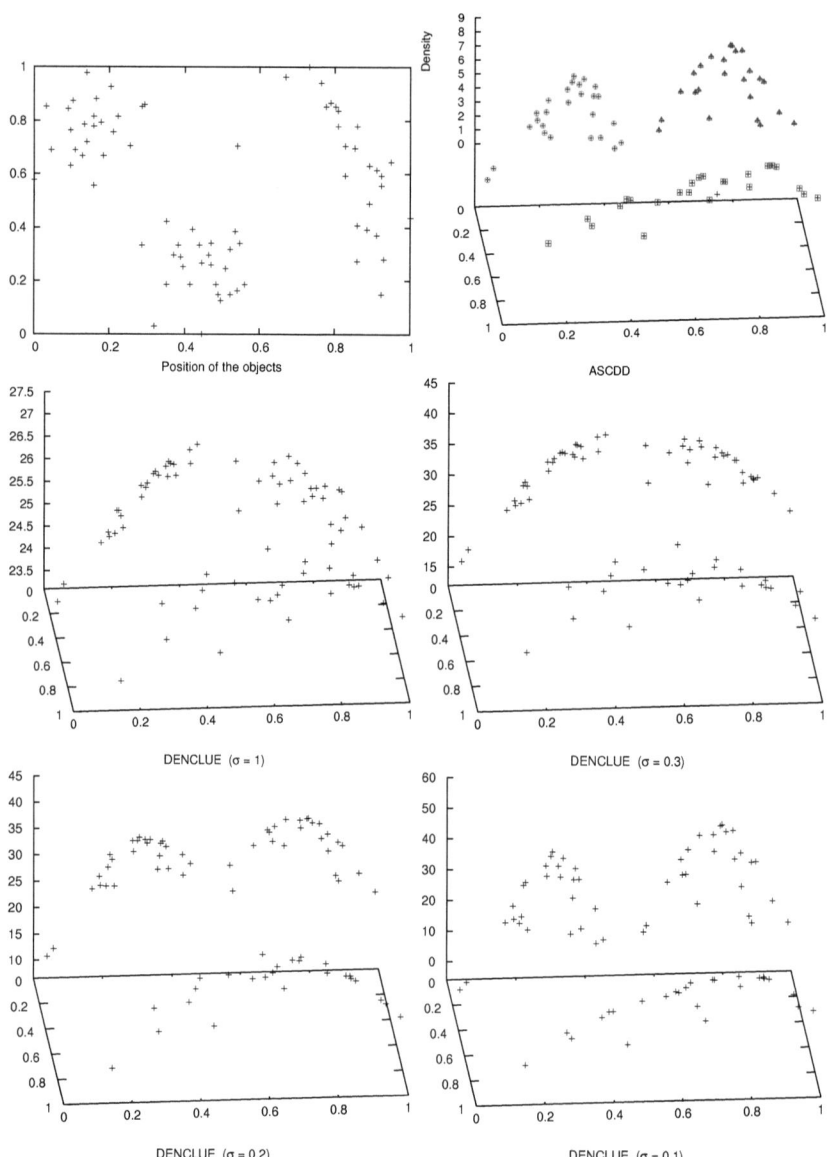

Figure 4.14: Comparison of ASCDD and DENCLUE

4.3 COMPARISON

4.3.4 ASCDD versus ENCLUS

Since the entropy is used by both ASCDD and ENCLUS [Chen 99] for detecting the potential subspace, we compare the clustering results of these two algorithms in this section.

As we introduced in section 2.2, ENCLUS calculates entropy based on the division of objects with grids. It needs interest gain defined in equation 2.3 to measure whether high-dimensional subspaces are strongly related. A subspace is considered as a potential subspace if its entropy is under a threshold ω and its interest gain exceeds another threshold ϵ'. In ASCDD, we use the maximal dimensionality (definition 3.18) to determine whether a subspace is "interesting". We will compare the differences of these two methods by applying them to the example mentioned in figure 3.9. The original data with 90 objects are listed in section 7.1.

Subspace	$N=5$ Entropy	Interest	Interest gain	$N=9$ Entropy	Interest	Interest gain	$N=12$ Entropy	Interest	Interest gain
$\{x\}$	1.261	0	0	1.544	0	0	1.894	0	0
$\{y\}$	1.260	0	0	1.641	0	0	1.672	0	0
$\{z\}$	1.278	0	0	1.589	0	0	1.696	0	0
$\{x,y\}$	2.060	0.461	0.461	2.531	0.654	0.654	2.872	0.694	0.694
$\{y,z\}$	2.035	0.503	0.503	2.594	0.636	0.636	2.631	0.737	0.737
$\{x,z\}$	2.046	0.493	0.493	2.589	0.544	0.544	2.758	0.832	0.832
$\{x,y,z\}$	2.653	1.146	0.643	3.350	1.424	0.770	3.603	1.659	0.827

Table 4.1: An example of entropy values calculated with ENCLUS

Table 4.1 shows the entropy, interest and interest gain calculated with the methods of ENCLUS. We choose the number of grid cells N for a one-dimensional subspace to be 5, 9 and 12. The result shows that the number of grid cells influences the entropy value of a subspace. The entropy becomes bigger as the

4. DISCUSSION & COMPARISON

number of grid cells increases, because when the number of cells grows, the objects spread out more equally throughout the entire cells than the objects placed in fewer grids.

One problem here is how to choose the parameter ω and ϵ' in order to select the potential subspaces. We set ω to 80% of the maximal entropy. The entropy of a one-dimensional subspace reaches the maximum value when the objects are evenly distributed within the N grids, which can be calculated with: $-N \cdot \frac{1}{N} \cdot \log(\frac{1}{N}) = -\log(\frac{1}{N}) = \log(N)$. Two- and three-dimensional subspaces have the maximal entropy values $\log(N^2)$ and $\log(N^3)$ respectively. For example, when N is set to 9, the parameters ω for the one-, two- and three-dimensional subspace are $0.8 \cdot \log(9) = 1.758$, $0.8 \cdot \log(81) = 3.516$ and $0.8 \cdot \log(729) = 5.237$. In this case, all subspaces are selected. However, it is still difficult to determine another threshold ϵ'. If we choose $\epsilon' = 0.5$, then $\{x, y\}$, $\{y, z\}$, $\{x, z\}$ and $\{x, y, z\}$ are all considered as potential subspaces. Finally, all subspaces are selected as "interesting". It is not wrong, but as we discussed for the example of figure 3.9, the two-dimensional subspaces have more distinct clusters than the three-dimensional subspace.

Subspace	$\{x\}$	$\{y\}$	$\{z\}$	$\{x, y\}$	$\{y, z\}$	$\{x, z\}$	$\{x, y, z\}$
Normalized entropy	0.982	0.983	0.986	0.946	0.952	0.948	0.993

Table 4.2: An example of entropy values calculated with ASCDD

Table 4.2 describes the entropy calculated by ASCDD. The calculation does not depend on any parameter. It is clear that the two-dimensional subspaces have lower entropy than the one- and three-dimensional subspaces. With the relation $E(x, y); E(y, z); E(x, z) < E(x); E(y); E(z) < E(x, y, z)$, the subspace $\{x, y\}$, $\{y, z\}$, $\{x, z\}$ are considered as the potential subspaces. In comparison with ENCLUS, the result of ASCDD corresponds much closer to the fact that the two-dimensional subspaces have more distinct clusters than the three-dimensional subspace.

4.4 Summary

In this chapter, we discussed issues and details about our subspace clustering methods SUGRA and ASCDD. It shows that both of them have some advantages and disadvantages.

SUGRA and ASCDD yielded clustering results with higher accuracy in comparison with other subspace clustering methods. Furthermore, the settings of parameters for SUGRA and ASCDD are relatively simple.

The next chapter illustrates more clustering results by showing empirical experiments on SUGRA and ASCDD and additional comparisons with other subspace clustering algorithms. The properties of SUGRA and ASCDD will be demonstrated more clearly through these experiments.

4. Discussion & Comparison

5
EMPIRICAL EXPERIMENTS

In this chapter, we show empirical experiments on the subspace clustering methods SUGRA and ASCDD and comparisons with other subspace clustering algorithms. Some experiments are already introduced in [Zhao 10a, Zhao 12, Zhao 13].

The purpose of these experiments is to observe the effectiveness and efficiency of SUGRA and ASCDD, particularly their accuracy and run time for large numbers of objects in high-dimensional spaces and their abilities for searching subspaces.

The experiments are carried out with both synthetic data and real data. We use the synthetic data as experimental data in order to make the experiments controllable and to measure the accuracy easily. The accuracy is defined as the proportion of the number of correctly clustered objects to the real number of objects in that cluster. The real data contains the data gathered from real situations, and is more complicated and more challenging for clustering than the synthetic data.

All experiments are carried out on a PC with 800MHz dual-core processor, 4GB RAM, Linux operating system and Java environment.

5. EMPIRICAL EXPERIMENTS

5.1 Experiments with SUGRA

5.1.1 Synthetic data

In the experiment with synthetic data, the results of SUGRA are compared with the subspace clustering method CLIQUE [Agra 98], because both methods are bottom-up subspace clustering methods.

Run time

In this experiment, we used a data set with a 10-dimensional space and five clusters in different subspaces. The number of objects was increased from 20000 to 160000 in different tests. Figure 5.1 shows that SUGRA has almost the same run time as CLIQUE. SUGRA is faster for a small number of objects but it requires more run time than CLIQUE for a large number of the objects. The reason is that the calculation of gravitation of an object in SUGRA involves all objects, so the run time of density calculation is quadratic. For a small number of objects, the calculation time is not influenced so strongly by the number of objects. However, a big number of objects can burden the CPU a lot.

In the next experiment, we used 10^5 objects as the test data. The number of dimensions increased from 10 to 60, where there were ten subspace clusters. Figure 5.2 indicates that SUGRA and CLIQUE require more run time as the number of dimension increases, which is similar to other bottom-up algorithms. The combination process will stop directly if there is no further cluster in a low-dimensional subspace, otherwise the combination process will continue in higher dimensions. SUGRA is faster than CLIQUE in this case, because SUGRA simply combines one-dimensional subspace clusters for searching high-dimensional clusters. Unlike SUGRA, CLIQUE has to check whether

5.1 EXPERIMENTS WITH SUGRA

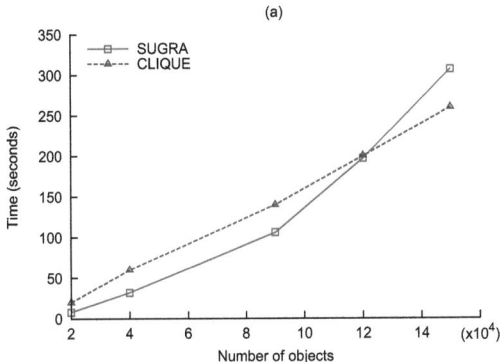

Figure 5.1: Run time (Objects) (SUGRA vs. CLIQUE)

high-dimensional cluster-combinations do still stay in the dense unit. Naturally the higher dimensionality of the subspace that the clusters are located in, the more time it requires. The pruning process of CLIQUE needs extra time, but this process is not necessary in SUGRA.

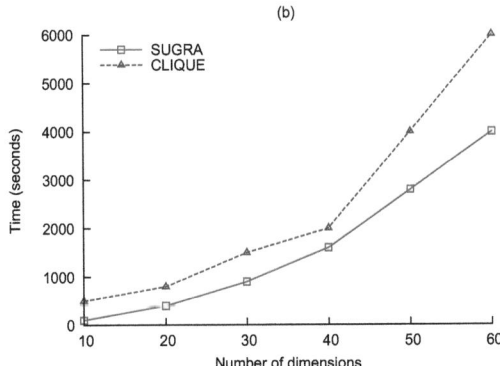

Figure 5.2: Run time (Dimension) (SUGRA vs. CLIQUE)

5. EMPIRICAL EXPERIMENTS

Accuracy

The accuracy of the clustering results is also an important evaluation for a clustering method. A test data set had 10^4 objects and 10-dimensional space with 5 clusters, which were divided in different subspaces.

Preset clusters	1	2	3	4	5
Subspace	{1,3,7,8,9}	{2,4,6,8}	{1,2,5,7,8,9,10}	{3,6,7,8,9}	{2,3,9,10}
Number of objects	2000	5000	1000	2000	3000
CLIQUE	{1,3,7,8,9} P: 0.64; R: 0.58	{2,6,8} P: 0.59; R: 0.64	{1,2,5,8,9} P: 0.56; R: 0.74	{3,6,7,8,9} P: 0.70; R: 0.72	{3,9,10} P: 0.41; R: 0.56
SUGRA	{1,3,7,8,9} P: 0.85; R: 0.86	{2,4,6,8} P: 0.90; R: 0.90	{1,2,5,7,8,9,10} P: 0.88; R: 0.96	{3,6,7,8,9} P: 0.92; R: 0.92	{2,3,9,10} P: 0.76; R: 0.81

(P: Precision; R: Recall)

Table 5.1: Comparison of clustering results from SUGRA and CLIQUE

The table 5.1 shows the clustering results of CLIQUE and SUGRA. CLIQUE finds sometimes fewer cluster objects and sometimes more cluster objects than the original number of cluster objects, because the grid-based method with partitioning and merging processes cause inaccuracies. For example, CLIQUE separates several clusters into small ones that are not considered as clusters, and the pruning process in CLIQUE can not merge these small ones together, because they are not clusters. Contrarily, the pruning process of CLIQUE can merge some non-cluster objects into the clusters, which can cause finding big clusters. In this experiment, the clustering result of SUGRA is more precise than CLIQUE, because SUGRA does not have this problem with partitioning and merging of a grid-based method. SUGRA does not have to separate the clusters into pieces but finds the clusters in one step by using the gravitation

5.1 EXPERIMENTS WITH SUGRA

threshold. The small inaccuracy with SUGRA comes from the vague objects on the verge of clusters.

5.1.2 Real data

Here we will show the clustering results of SUGRA and CLIQUE on two real data sets.

"Iris"

The data set "Iris"[1] was obtained from the UC Irvine Machine Learning Repository [Bach 13]. It includes 150 objects and 4 attributes. The attributes are: sepal length (a_1), sepal width (a_2), petal length (a_3) and petal width (a_4). The data set contains three clusters, where each cluster has 50 objects and refers to a type of iris plant: Iris Setosa (S_1), Iris Versicolour (S_2) and Iris Virginica (S_3). Figure 5.3 illustrates the gravitation calculation with SUGRA on four attributes.

Iris	clusters	S_1	S_2	S_3
	objects	1-50	51-100	101-150
CLIQUE	subspace	{3,4}	{1,2,3,4}	
	objects	P: 0.95; R: 0.93	P: 0.69; R: 0.46	
SUGRA	subspace	{2,3,4}	{1,2,4}	{2,4}
	objects	P: 1; R: 1	P: 0.90; R: 0.94	P: 0.89; R: 0.82

(P: Precision; R: Recall)

Table 5.2: Accuracy of SUGRA on "iris"

---
[1] http://archive.ics.uci.edu/ml/datasets/Iris

5. EMPIRICAL EXPERIMENTS

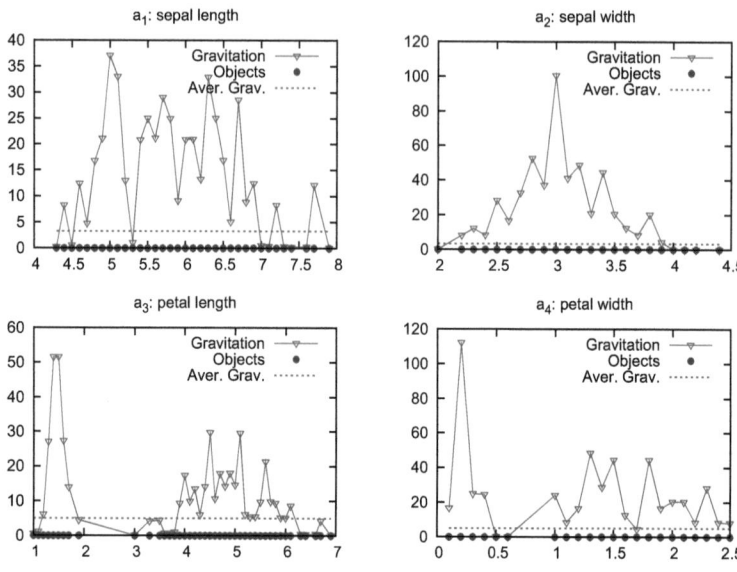

Figure 5.3: Gravitation of the four attributes on "iris"

The clustering results of SUGRA and CLIQUE are shown in table 5.2. CLIQUE was set with 5 grids on each subspace and density threshold $\tau = 20\%$. The cluster S_1 is easily discovered by both SUGRA and CLIQUE, because S_1 is far from the other two clusters, especially in the dimensions a_3 and a_4. Clusters S_2 and S_3 are mixed, because some boundary objects are not very clear (in a_3 near 5.3, in a_4 near 1.7). At these two places, the objects should be separated. However, the gravitation values with SUGRA are not low enough with the gravitation threshold of 3.29 to separate them. In this situation, we increased the gravitation threshold on a_3 and a_4 with $\overline{G^{a_3}} = 5$, $\overline{G^{a_4}} = 5$. CLIQUE can not separate the clusters S_2 and S_3 even when the parameters are changed, so it retains them as one cluster. Changing the parameter in CLIQUE usually causes

5.1 Experiments with SUGRA

that the clusters disappear or connect as one big cluster. Although the clustering results of S_2 and S_3 with SUGRA are a little different from the original clusters, the clustering results of these two clusters have still high precision.

"Wine"

Another data set "wine"[1] was also obtained from [Bach 13]. The data represent the results of a chemical analysis of wines grown in the same region in Italy but were derived from three different cultivars. The analysis determined the quantities of 13 constituents found in each of the three types of wines. There are 178 objects and 13 attributes in this data set.

Wine (dimension)	a_1	a_2	a_3	a_4	a_5	a_6	a_7	a_8	a_9	a_{10}	a_{11}	a_{12}	a_{13}
Threshold	3	2	5	5	3.29	2.3	2	3.29	3.29	3.29	2.2	2	2

Table 5.3: Threshold setting for SUGRA on "wine"

The three types of wines are three clusters that are distributed in $\{o_1, \ldots, o_{59}\}$, $\{o_{60}, \ldots, o_{130}\}$ and $\{o_{131}, \ldots, o_{178}\}$. Because there are too many subspace clusters within different subspaces, the results can not be listed here. The accuracy of the clustering results with CLIQUE is 68%, 62%, 75% for the three clusters. In order to get a higher accuracy, we altered the thresholds for some subspaces. The selected thresholds of each dimension are listed in table 5.3, where the thresholds are all around 3.29. SUGRA has then the accuracy with 74%, 65%, 85%.

Altering the gravitation threshold in SUGRA has generally the following principles: If the objects in a dimension trends to be uniformly distributed, the threshold can be chosen with the value lower than 3.29. Contrarily, a threshold bigger than 3.29 can be used for clusters with unclear boundaries.

---
[1] http://archive.ics.uci.edu/ml/datasets/Wine

5.2 Experiments on ASCDD

In this section, we show the experiments on ASCDD with synthetic and real data. The clustering results will also compared with other subspace clustering methods.

5.2.1 Synthetic Data

"Galaxy"

The synthetic data in this experiment was a manually defined "galaxy stars". The data set has 8372 objects with two dimensions. The experimental data and clustering result are shown in figure 5.4, where the cluster objects are marked with different colors and the black objects are outliers. We set $q = 0.97$ as the parameter setting. The clustering process required 72 seconds. The clustering result shows great accuracy according to our expectation on both concave and convex shaped clusters.

Figure 5.5 illustrates the densities of objects in three-dimensional space. The axis z shows that all objects have densities from 0 to 900. The curve of the density function presents the distribution of the objects very clearly: The outliers (black color) have very low density values that are close to 0; The start objects have much higher densities than the edge objects.

We also applied this data set to the clustering algorithm DENCLUE, which uses the Gaussian kernel function to estimate the density. We set the two parameters of DENCLUE with $\xi = 2$ and $\epsilon = 0.7$, it required 106 seconds to finish the clustering process. The clustering result shows that some clusters are found correctly, for instance the cluster with red color. However, since not all the clusters in this data set have the Gaussian distribution, DENCLUE can not

5.2 EXPERIMENTS ON ASCDD

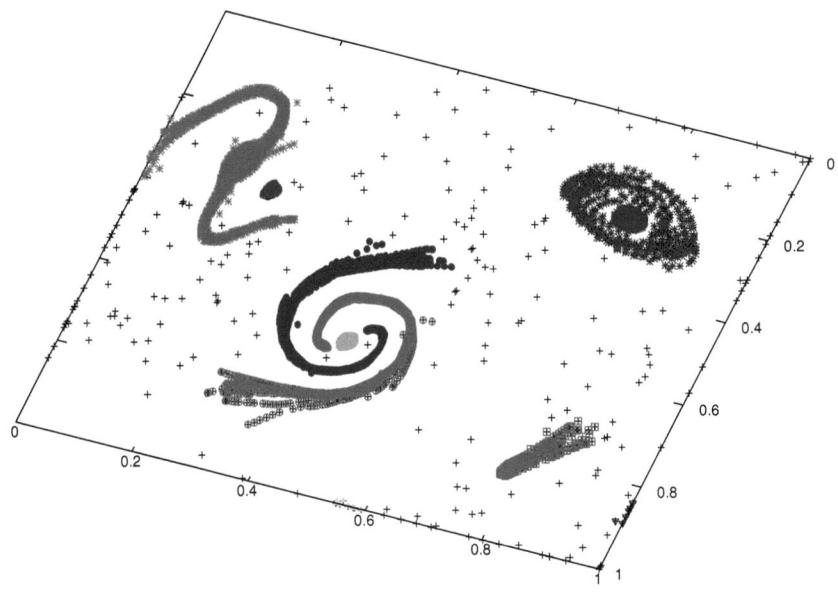

Figure 5.4: Clustering result of "Galaxy" with ASCDD

find some clusters correctly. For example, the three clusters with spiral shapes (blue) are found as one cluster by DENCLUE, which can not be changed by adjusting the parameters.

Run time with different q

In the next experiment, a synthetic data set consisted of 10^4 objects and 100 dimensions. 20 clusters with different shapes were hidden in 10 different subspaces. The subspaces without clusters were filled with random objects.

We compared the results of ASCDD with different settings of the parameter DDT. As we defined in definition 3.20, DDT depends on q, determining the DDT means choosing the $q \in (0, 1)$. The two extreme situations $q = 0$ and

5. EMPIRICAL EXPERIMENTS

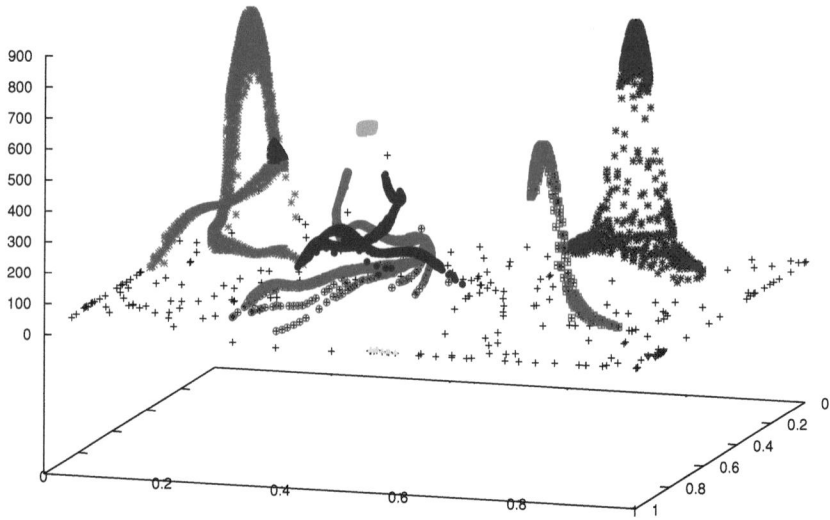

Figure 5.5: Clustering result of "Galaxy" with ASCDD demonstrated in 3D

$q = 1$ cause two results: no cluster object and one cluster with the entire objects. As we discussed in section 4.2.1, bigger clusters can be found with a q close to 1 than with a small q. Moreover, more objects are explored as cluster objects than that with a small q. Contrarily, when q approximates to 0, some small clusters disappear, and the big clusters shrink to small ones. However, the computation time will be reduced with a small q, because many small clusters will not be dense on high-dimensional subspaces anymore, which means it saves the searching time in these subspaces. Generally speaking, altering q between 1 and 0 could adjust between details of clusters and run time. Figure 5.6 presents the run time with four arbitrarily chosen q values. The run time becomes longer when q and the number of objects increase.

5.2 EXPERIMENTS ON ASCDD

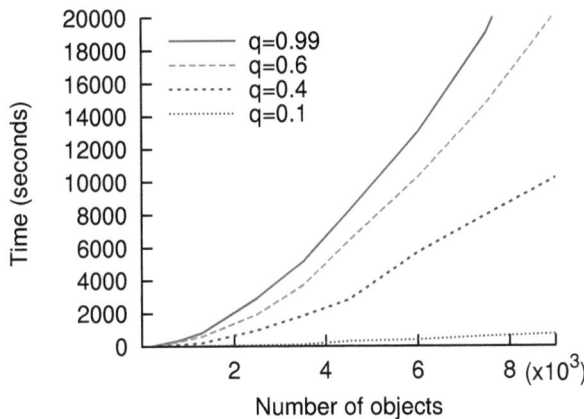

Figure 5.6: Run time with different q

Comparison with ENCLUS

Since ENCLUS [Chen 99] is one of the most famous subspace clustering methods by applying entropy, we compared ASCDD with ENCLUS in the next experiment with regard to potential subspaces and clustering results. The data set used for this experiment contained 70 dimensions and 10^4 objects. There were 25 clusters within 15 different subspaces.

ASCDD starts searching with the subspace with lowest entropy, and expands the subspace to its maximal dimensionality. The process of searching potential subspace works automatically, which does not need parameters. Finally ASCDD finds all expected subspaces and some extra subspaces.

We applied ENCLUS by setting the number of units to 285 in order to keep averagely 35 objects in each cell as the authors suggest. ENCLUS needs ω and ϵ as thresholds of parameters *entropy* and *interest gain* for detecting interesting subspace. However, it is a challenge to choose proper values for these two parameters. We chose $\omega = 8.5$, $\epsilon = 1$ as described in the article. ENCLUS did not

5. EMPIRICAL EXPERIMENTS

find all the possible subspace, ENCLUS found only part of expected subspaces and some non-expected subspaces. Even by altering the two parameters with different combinations, the result of interesting subspaces with of ENCLUS were still mixed with non-expected subspaces.

Next we compared the clustering results between ASCDD and ENCLUS. ENCLUS uses grid-based method by searching the clusters firstly in one-dimensional subspace, and combines the clusters in high-dimensional subspace to search more clusters. In this experiment, we chose the same parameters as the above paragraph. ENCLUS found just some simple low-dimensional convex clusters correctly. In high-dimensional subspace, ENCLUS showed much inaccuracy because some concave clusters are bound together as one cluster and some are separated into small clusters. Unlike ENCLUS, ASCDD can focus directly on the high-dimensional subspace for searching clusters. In parameter setting of ASCDD, we chose $q = 0.9$, which is very close to 1. ASCDD found the clusters with both convex and concave shapes with high precision.

The efficiency evaluation of ASCDD and ENCLUS are illustrated in figure 5.7. We used subsets of the synthetic data for this evaluation. ASCDD and ENCLUS used the same parameter settings as stated above.

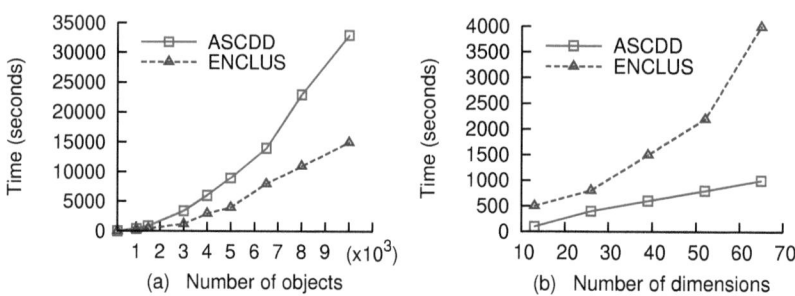

Figure 5.7: ASCDD compared with ENCLUS

5.2 EXPERIMENTS ON ASCDD

Figure 5.7 (a) presents that the run time of ASCDD grows quadratically with increasing number of objects because the density calculation of each object involves all the objects. Although the run time of ASCDD with regard to the number of objects is not linear, the complexity ensures ASCDD gets more accurate clustering results than ENCLUS, whose clustering results are often bigger or smaller than the original clusters. Of course the run time with regard to the number of objects depends also on the parameter settings, for example it requires more run time in ASCDD by choosing the parameter DDT that yields many objects in clusters than a DDT that involves few objects.

As shown in figure 5.7 (b), the run time of ASCDD increases linearly as the number of dimensions grows. The reason is that ASCDD searches firstly only the potential subspace, and the clustering process executes directly on each high-dimensional potential subspace. ASCDD has almost the same run time for a clustering within a subspace with high or low dimensionality. ENCLUS is slower than ASCDD for high-dimensional subspace because ENCLUS does clustering only from low to high-dimensional subspace, which requires much time than direct clustering in high-dimensional subspace as ASCDD.

Comparison with SUBCLU

SUBCLU [Krog 04] is a density-based bottom-up subspace clustering algorithm, which uses the technique of DBSCAN [Este 96]. SUBCLU starts clustering from one-dimensional subspace, and then checks whether the higher-dimensional subspace clusters combined from low-dimensional subspace clusters are still dense. The main differences between SUBCLU and ASCDD with regard to the neighborhood-expansion process are as follows: SUBCLU needs two parameters the minimum distance ϵ and the minimum number $minPts$ for finding the start object and searching density-connected objects, where ASCDD finds automatically the start object and needs one parameter DDT for expanding the neighbors.

We applied the same synthetic data set on ASCDD and SUBCLU in order to compare the performances of the two algorithms. The first experiment data set had ten dimensions with the same value ranges and 10^3 objects. In the first test, we set five simple clusters in different subspaces. By choosing the proper parameters, both algorithms yielded almost the same results. Both methods found the five clusters. The run time is also similar for two methods. It is noteworthy that as the dimensionality of subspace increases, the parameter settings are changing. The setting of ϵ and $minPts$ for SUBCLU is quite difficult by high-dimensional subspace, whereas the parameter DDT of ASCDD is relatively simple to choose because q should always be selected between 0 and 1 and possibly close to 1.

In the next experiment, we changed the ten-dimensional data with various value ranges. In this case, SUBCLU can not continue to work in the subspace that is higher than four dimension, because in high-dimensional subspaces all objects appear to be sparse, and the strategy of choosing neighborhood with the minimum distance ϵ becomes less efficient. Another problem is that it is difficult to choose the proper ϵ for various value ranges. However, ASCDD worked still excellent in this situation, and did not have troubles in discovering the five subspace clusters.

5.2.2 Real Data

"Wine"

In this experiment, we used the data set "wine"[1] [Bach 13] again for AS-

---
[1] http://archive.ics.uci.edu/ml/datasets/Wine

5.2 EXPERIMENTS ON ASCDD

CDD, which was already used for SUGRA. The data set corresponds to the analysis of wines derived from three different cultivars. There are 13 dimensions with three clusters (with 59, 71 and 48 objects). Each dimension measures a constituent of the three types of wines.

The clusters were detected by ASCDD in many subspaces. We illustrate two examples of the clustering results and their accuracies in table 5.4. For instance, by applying ASCDD directly on the 13 dimensional space, we found two subspace clusters S_1, S_2, where S_1 corresponds to the original clusters S_a and S_b together, and S_2 corresponds to S_c. The clustering required 0.05 seconds. In the second example, we found three clusters S_3, S_4 and S_5 on the subspace $\{3, 7, 12, 13\}$. The accuracy of each cluster is shown in the table. This clustering process required 0.04 seconds.

Subspace	Clusters (P: Precision; R: Recall)		
$\mathcal{A} = \{1, \cdots, 13\}$	S_1 (P: 0.70; R: 0.58)	S_2 (P: 0.86; R: 0.82)	
$\mathcal{A} = \{3, 7, 12, 13\}$	S_3 (P: 0.82; R: 0.71)	S_4 (P: 0.64; R: 0.43)	S_5 (P: 0.90; R: 0.88)

Table 5.4: Result of ASCDD on "wine".

The clustering results of ASCDD are quite close to the original clusters. The clustering process of ASCDD can be implemented directly on high-dimensional subspaces, and furthermore the run time for high-dimensional subspaces is still very low.

We compared the clustering result of ASCDD with FINDIT [Woo 04], which is a partition-based subspace clustering approach. Since we knew already the number of clusters, it simplified applying FINDIT. In the parameter setting of

FINDIT, we chose 40 for the minimum number of objects in a cluster and 1.3 for the minimum distance between two clusters. FINDIT required 2 seconds to finish the clustering process, and found similar clusters as ASCDD did. However, if we changed the number of clusters to a different value, the clustering results of FINDIT were then very different.

"Gas sensor array drift"

From the UC Irvine Machine Learning Repository [Bach 13] we obtained the data set "Gas Sensor Array Drift"[1]. The data set corresponds to the measurements of 16 chemical sensors utilized in simulations for drift compensation in discriminating six gas types (Ammonia, Acetaldehyde, Acetone, Ethylene, Ethanol, and Toluene) at various concentrations. The data is prepared for the chemo-sensor research community and artificial intelligence to develop strategies to cope with sensor/concept drift. The data set contains 128 dimensions, 13910 measurements with six gas types (six clusters). The task is to find the combinations of chemical elements that can detect the gas types. We applied both ASCDD and ENCLUS on the data without cluster labels, the results were then compared with the original cluster labels.

We illustrate some examples of the clustering results related to months one and two in table 5.5.

This clustering process required 1440 seconds with ASCDD and 4410 seconds with ENCLUS. Compared with ENCLUS, ASCDD is more efficient and has higher precision in high-dimensional subspace clustering than ENCLUS.

---

[1]http://archive.ics.uci.edu/ml/datasets/Gas+Sensor+Array+Drift+Dataset

5.2 EXPERIMENTS ON ASCDD

Cluster	ASCDD Precision	Subspace	ENCLUS Precision	Subspace
1	68%	76, 113, 17, 4, 79, 70, 14, 68, 121, 57, 15, 6, 7, 53, 118, 12, 54, 62, 127	41%	113, 4, 79, 70, 68, 57, 15, 54, 7, 14, 53, 118, 83, 14, 73
2	67%	15, 6, 78, 49, 7, 12, 55, 63	55%	20, 6, 78, 30, 19, 7, 66, 23, 11, 50, 93
3	39%	47, 24, 107, 111, 88, 97, 99, 105	31%	88, 40, 26, 113, 105, 95, 33, 28, 16
4	68%	44, 108, 39, 47, 24, 103, 111, 88, 97, 99, 105	52%	111, 23, 108, 75, 39, 94, 47, 85
5	34%	112, 56, 120, 122, 98, 16, 35, 106, 43, 80, 36, 108, 24, 107, 88, 97, 99, 105	19%	112, 43, 106, 16, 80, 24, 74, 87, 86, 98, 19, 108, 58
6	88%	65, 9, 76, 4, 79, 70, 14, 68, 15, 6, 78, 7, 12, 39, 47, 103	59%	65, 83, 4, 68, 70, 6, 81, 14, 7, 103, 79

Table 5.5: Results of ASCDD and ENCLUS on "Gas Sensor Array Drift"

6
CONCLUSION

This dissertation proposes and characterizes two subspace clustering algorithms SUGRA (Subspace Clustering with the Gravitation Function) [Zhao 10a] and ASCDD (Automatic Subspace Clustering with the Distance -Density Function) [Zhao 12, Zhao 13]. Since most subspace clustering methods suffer from the issue that it is troublesome to determine their parameters, the purpose of our studies is to simplify the settings of parameters in order to facilitate the application of subspace clustering methods in practice.

Our new method SUGRA applies the gravitation function in order to calculate the density of objects. An important property of SUGRA is that the non-cluster objects have density values smaller than a threshold. Meanwhile, the cluster objects have much larger values than this threshold. The threshold has approximately a value of 3.29, which does not depend on the number of objects. SUGRA follows a bottom-up clustering process, which searches firstly each one-dimensional subspace, and then checks the combinations of low-dimensional subspace clusters in high-dimensional subspaces.

The second method ASCDD calculates also the density of objects. However, ASCDD uses a different density function than SUGRA and applies many other techniques in the clustering process, such as expanding neighborhood and exploring potential subspaces with entropy. The neighborhood expansion ensures finding subspace clusters with any shapes. A low entropy value of a subspace

6. CONCLUSION

indicates that the subspace is potential for finding clusters. ASCDD detects firstly the maximal dimensionality of potential subspaces and then searches the clusters directly in each potential subspace. The process of searching potential subspaces is automatic, and the neighborhood expansion needs only one parameter, which has the range $[0, 1]$.

The comparison and empirical experiments indicate that SUGRA and ASCDD can be easily applied to data with different value ranges. Furthermore, these two methods yield clustering results with higher accuracy than other subspace clustering methods but require only a simple setting of parameters. SUGRA can be used in many cases by choosing the threshold 3.29. However, the threshold can be slightly adjusted in some situations in order to get higher accuracy. ASCDD can identify clusters with arbitrary shapes. The clusters are detected by ASCDD according to their densities, which does not depend on the input order. The parameter required by ASCDD in the neighborhood expansion is simple. It usually can be chosen close to its maximum value in order to yield clusters.

The main limitation of our study is that the run time grows quadratically as the number of objects increases, because in both SUGRA and ASCDD, the calculation of the density value of an object involves all objects. The future research will be focused on optimizing the run time, for example, random sampling can be used instead of the entire set of objects in the density calculation in order to improve the speed with a very large number of objects.

Another future study could be the adaption of the subspace clustering methods to various data types, such as time series or multimedia data.

7
APPENDIXES

7.1 Appendix A

The following table lists the three-dimensional data set related to figure 3.9.

x	y	z
0.4730011283192138	0.9612102957898717	0.6282110694166531
0.508530770154819	0.9932858325537071	0.9349343098204828
0.507159219817764	0.97512902789024	0.09930613037703816
0.5127140442140167	0.9779671453351743	0.4757685887350595
0.5031532991992841	0.9966260021560709	0.7356774968244953
0.47591506758845104	0.9986654255834072	0.7190634042491406
0.5035207600484914	0.9758924994997382	0.16252400995503288
0.4643599223914509	0.9618726794501848	0.271084880847213
0.4568761413668097	0.9889462439660984	0.2219110200867313
0.4838620439503893	0.9681637091124196	0.3292234976252114
0.509498169935583	0.9832239145062116	0.2053228376835948
0.49529932035642377	0.9866977264710048	0.9517132635872769
0.4633555487500571	0.9899051730422	0.8492228328292082
0.5053657283122357	0.945596389650087	0.6045889245696863
0.4738526977513474	0.9751347565568873	0.5996544984560435
0.5093214082857972	0.9971422573831376	0.347604648058783
0.49217626098665745	0.9889283968930445	0.9361214061825179
0.4831018833349414	1.0	0.31335399558504246
0.458676394690458	0.9540242202907606	0.3594228059778682
		Continued on next page

7. APPENDIXES

x	y	z
0.5022169779628294	0.958527094124501	0.5100317945056634
0.5079761076415037	0.990062628603441	0.3842755830823454
0.46725301961648613	0.9782975670472382	0.5160619599367016
0.4816749384747505	0.9929591879975602	0.3008959160267451
0.5122362112572396	0.9597850025786459	0.5208504275223238
0.46338750957247005	0.9616317850264011	0.0
0.5028737908569963	0.964906804497335	0.9399149858691653
0.5016854167955148	0.9873716104380567	0.9001168418055306
0.4863741555107523	0.976090316458028	0.6020468120965289
0.4755768132410899	0.9904603605767763	0.24329429006551104
0.4923010438136428	0.9481730426639245	0.1882387275501861
0.9585229093044194	0.06580888484018996	0.4861649430808801
0.9776610210421223	0.70444839037419	0.4482510357027089
1.0	0.03119459184350662	0.4376289332934707
0.9778549822865452	0.0	0.48384744865521584
0.994529384411328	0.42389100919865336	0.4945921500635462
0.9904282761361972	0.5617949995990943	0.4819996011317272
0.9851114743533554	0.9095942485089805	0.47408722669776676
0.9570279973312904	0.3486083215829756	0.4560264872382409
0.9683309722252635	0.5983236829877193	0.4368395633682064
0.982739456184984	0.8232493619246947	0.4590110742269297
0.9695698323426947	0.35752489919673897	0.4583167155393761
0.9722806400026927	0.20736507512636423	0.458699396669012016
0.9849036918052428	0.9615892517347563	0.4749214928098718
0.9920838949649954	0.06605109725329868	0.47805085130670644
0.9665191631079211	0.9194689930494531	0.49006852736700995
0.9717696549847662	0.22610151099294906	0.4910606996292407
0.9537364723346974	0.39800596108679026	0.46613468605332986
0.9876145688075029	0.9347268201516857	0.4534647933587315
0.9989707887813511	0.12999745887851102	0.47143781964503306
0.9479410726349033	0.7786314433240971	0.434828069513582
0.9648759013337348	0.17449326285291938	0.44109559244661734
0.9951759006360101	0.8512233597121897	0.4788182254447671
		Continued on next page

7.1 APPENDIX A

x	y	z
0.9754113735361141	0.9085429667684816	0.488218690409371
0.9900145332761915	0.9412410467591643	0.4495447907275556
0.9692350056540515	0.680030021533559	0.4821963362009923
0.9470506187862608	0.4304676643104892	0.45689871781096797
0.9646363390200567	0.2849239267015102	0.4614564524347223
0.9900458701350155	0.32081609078424767	0.47367099125566126
0.9522181830320228	0.1819989671014806	0.4858378709204199
0.9503325552084042	0.315608771324952	0.4817262858948488
0.4692376401568368	0.4623103924698122	0.9975419553641346
0.6746333872638749	0.48641216311268404	0.9904959757337198
0.5319468028068531	0.4806140567232098	0.990241255483499
0.7165163435361294	0.4925361468366189	0.9777605905565022
0.4153825252341009	0.48860989788682885	0.986032174530355
0.6573980482017492	0.46088944118778064	0.9464303573450801
0.5922114959232897	0.4589549186556198	0.986297214197329
0.08007290894939786	0.475075626974711	0.9458660814237905
0.9291246254553452	0.4665533157738916	0.98968898227394
0.012872718231806184	0.45978597068176164	0.991525621238826
0.0693802950927522	0.4918267413459769	0.9619629924630341
0.6009599794218656	0.4412988185122136	1.0
0.9003130242087116	0.4453608615259125	0.9805057237222492
0.8026940953525877	0.481785323129864	0.9523920960628272
0.2557498815499801	0.48269637606060056	0.9656443700267326
0.9588887661917795	0.4415232811864237	0.9557634006436856
0.14226053318167542	0.4702943716613444	0.9440271927002727
0.2307031337022026	0.4497523607936268	0.9945053500498834
0.9152803973049509	0.4852110842490298	0.9443917219267656
0.40484187610411415	0.498052847957586	0.9419394600450518
0.0725428482364476	0.47566170159492865	0.9820479806375346
0.47388378548445537	0.4862228316475461	0.9888082842742297
0.7181430578236923	0.4586210840408313	0.9890579150266778
0.14320516015044923	0.44105489013554794	0.9435822902312655
0.9621104320068049	0.49336825461817213	0.9718645152914294
		Continued on next page

x	y	z
0.7920804935126288	0.49798031796882924	0.9455194320726596
0.6486566607496604	0.485701541389139	0.959342657916061
0.0	0.495040667269766	0.9999982017900144
0.3837386428368687	0.4509870018903454	0.9792500316660431
0.11399916806170969	0.4663723378332479	0.9472228585310871

Table 7.1: A three dimensional data set

REFERENCES

[Agga 00] C. C. Aggarwal and P. S. Yu. "Finding generalized projected clusters in high dimensional spaces". In: *Proceedings of the 2000 ACM SIGMOD international conference on Management of data*, pp. 70–81, ACM, 2000. 16, 22

[Agga 99] C. C. Aggarwal, J. L. Wolf, P. S. Yu, C. Procopiuc, and J. S. Park. "Fast algorithms for projected clustering". In: *Proceedings of the 1999 ACM SIGMOD international conference on Management of data*, pp. 61–72, ACM, 1999. 16, 22

[Agra 05] R. Agrawal, J. Gehrke, D. Gunopulos, and P. Raghavan. "Automatic Subspace Clustering of High Dimensional Data". *Data Min. Knowl. Discov.*, Vol. 11, No. 1, pp. 5–33, July 2005.

[Agra 98] R. Agrawal, J. Gehrke, D. Gunopulos, and P. Raghavan. "Automatic subspace clustering of high dimensional data for data mining applications". In: *Proceedings of the 1998 ACM SIGMOD international conference on Management of data*, pp. 94–105, ACM, 1998. 16, 17, 18, 77, 86

[Air 57] U. S. D. of the Air Force. *Noise guide for air base commanders. Air Force pamphlet*, The Department, 1957. 1

[Anke 99] M. Ankerst, M. M. Breunig, H.-P. Kriegel, and J. Sander. "OPTICS: ordering points to identify the clustering structure". *SIGMOD Rec.*, Vol. 28, No. 2, pp. 49–60, June 1999.

REFERENCES

[Asse 08] I. Assent, R. Krieger, E. Müller, and T. Seidl. "EDSC: efficient density-based subspace clustering". In: *Proceedings of the 17th ACM conference on Information and knowledge management*, pp. 1093–1102, ACM, New York, NY, USA, 2008.

[Bach 13] K. Bache and M. Lichman. "UCI Machine Learning Repository". http://archive.ics.uci.edu/ml, 2013. 89, 91, 98, 100

[Bell 03] R. Bellman. *Dynamic Programming. Dover Books on Mathematics*, Dover, 2003. 3, 11, 31

[Berk 02] P. Berkhin. "Survey Of Clustering Data Mining Techniques". Tech. Rep., Accrue Software, Inc., 2002.

[Beye 99] K. S. Beyer, J. Goldstein, R. Ramakrishnan, and U. Shaft. "When Is "Nearest Neighbor" Meaningful?". In: *Proceedings of the 7th International Conference on Database Theory*, pp. 217–235, Springer-Verlag, London, UK, 1999. 3, 11, 31

[Bezd 81] J. C. Bezdek. *Pattern recognition with fuzzy objective function algorithms*. Kluwer Academic Publishers, 1981. 15

[Bohm 00] C. Böhm, B. Braunmüller, M. Breunig, and H.-P. Kriegel. "High performance clustering based on the similarity join". In: *Proceedings of the ninth international conference on Information and knowledge management*, pp. 298–305, ACM, New York, NY, USA, 2000.

[Bohm 04] C. Bohm, K. Railing, H.-P. Kriegel, and P. Kroger. "Density connected clustering with local subspace preferences". In: *Data Min-*

REFERENCES

ing, 2004. ICDM'04. Fourth IEEE International Conference on, pp. 27–34, IEEE, 2004. 21

[Chan 02] J.-W. Chang and D.-S. Jin. "A new cell-based clustering method for large, high-dimensional data in data mining applications". In: *Proceedings of the 2002 ACM symposium on Applied computing*, pp. 503–507, ACM, 2002. 16, 20

[Chen 12] X. Chen, Y. Ye, X. Xu, and J. Z. Huang. "A feature group weighting method for subspace clustering of high-dimensional data". *Pattern Recogn.*, Vol. 45, No. 1, pp. 434–446, Jan. 2012.

[Chen 99] C.-H. Cheng, A. W. Fu, and Y. Zhang. "Entropy-based subspace clustering for mining numerical data". In: *Proceedings of the fifth ACM SIGKDD international conference on Knowledge discovery and data mining*, pp. 84–93, ACM, 1999. 16, 19, 50, 81, 95

[Chu 09] Y.-H. Chu, Y.-J. Chen, D.-N. Yang, and M.-S. Chen. "Reducing Redundancy in Subspace Clustering". *IEEE Trans. on Knowl. and Data Eng.*, Vol. 21, No. 10, pp. 1432–1446, Oct. 2009.

[Date 05] C. Date. *Database in Depth*. O'Reilly, May 2005.

[Demp 77] A. P. Dempster, N. M. Laird, and D. B. Rubin. "Maximum likelihood from incomplete data via the EM algorithm". *Journal of the Royal Statistical Society. Series B (Methodological)*, pp. 1–38, 1977. 12

[Deng 10] Z. Deng, K.-S. Choi, F.-L. Chung, and S. Wang. "Enhanced soft subspace clustering integrating within-cluster and between-cluster

REFERENCES

information". *Pattern Recogn.*, Vol. 43, No. 3, pp. 767–781, March 2010.

[Deng 11] Z. Deng, K.-S. Choi, F.-L. Chung, and S. Wang. "EEW-SC: Enhanced Entropy-Weighting Subspace Clustering for high dimensional gene expression data clustering analysis". *Appl. Soft Comput.*, Vol. 11, No. 8, pp. 4798–4806, Dec. 2011.

[Este 96] M. Ester, H.-P. Kriegel, J. Sander, and X. Xu. "A density-based algorithm for discovering clusters in large spatial databases with noise". In: *Proceedings of the 2nd International Conference on Knowledge Discovery and Data mining*, pp. 226–231, AAAI Press, 1996. 9, 21, 58, 97

[Esti 02] V. Estivill-Castro. "Why so many clustering algorithms: a position paper". *SIGKDD Explor. Newsl.*, Vol. 4, No. 1, pp. 65–75, June 2002. 5

[Fayy 96] U. Fayyad, G. Piatetsky-shapiro, and P. Smyth. "From Data Mining to Knowledge Discovery in Databases". *AI Magazine*, Vol. 17, pp. 37–54, 1996.

[Forc 99] K. Forcht and K. Cochran. "Using data mining and datawarehousing techniques". *Industrial Management & Data Systems*, Vol. 99, No. 5, pp. 189–196, 1999.

[Fral 98] C. Fraley and A. E. Raftery. "How Many Clusters? Which Clustering Method? Answers Via Model-Based Cluster Analysis". *The Computer Journal*, Vol. 41, No. 8, pp. 578–588, 1998.

REFERENCES

[Frie 04] J. H. Friedman and J. J. Meulman. "Clustering objects on subsets of attributes". *Journal of the Royal Statistical Society: Series B (Statistical Methodology)*, pp. 815–849, 2004. 16

[Fua 99] Y.-H. Fua, M. O. Ward, and E. A. Rundensteiner. "Hierarchical parallel coordinates for exploration of large datasets". In: *Proceedings of the conference on Visualization '99*, pp. 43–50, 1999.

[Gan 04] G. Gan and J. Wu. "Subspace clustering for high dimensional categorical data". *SIGKDD Explor. Newsl.*, Vol. 6, No. 2, pp. 87–94, Dec. 2004.

[Goil 99] S. Goil, H. Nagesh, and A. Choudhary. "Mafia: Efficient and scalable subspace clustering for very large data sets". Technical Report CPDC-TR-9906-010, Northwestern University, 1999. 16, 20

[Gome 03] J. Gomez, D. Dasgupta, and O. Nasraoui. "A New Gravitational Clustering Algorithm". In: *In Proc. of the SIAM Int. Conf. on Data Mining (SDM)*, 2003.

[Grah 03] M. Graham and J. Kennedy. "Using Curves to Enhance Parallel Coordinate Visualisations". In: *IV '03: Proceedings of the Seventh International Conference on Information Visualization*, p. 10, IEEE Computer Society, 2003.

[Gunn 11] S. Günnemann, I. Färber, E. Müller, I. Assent, and T. Seidl. "External evaluation measures for subspace clustering". In: *Proceedings of the 20th ACM international conference on Information and knowledge management*, pp. 1363–1372, ACM, New York, NY, USA, 2011.

REFERENCES

[Han 06] J. Han and M. Kamber. *Data Mining: Concepts and Techniques*. Morgan Kaufmann, second Ed., 2006. 5, 9

[Hinn 03] A. Hinneburg and D. A. Keim. "A General Approach to Clustering in Large Databases with Noise". *Knowledge and Information Systems*, Vol. 5, No. 4, pp. 387–415, 2003.

[Hinn 07] A. Hinneburg and H.-H. Gabriel. "DENCLUE 2.0: fast clustering based on kernel density estimation". In: *Proceedings of the 7th international conference on Intelligent data analysis*, pp. 70–80, Springer-Verlag, 2007. 14

[Hinn 98] A. Hinneburg, E. Hinneburg, and D. A. Keim. "An Efficient Approach to Clustering in Large Multimedia Databases with Noise". In: *Proc. 4rd Int. Conf. on Knowledge Discovery and Data Mining*, pp. 58–65, AAAI Press, 1998. 12, 13, 79, 123

[Huan 97] Z. Huang. "A Fast Clustering Algorithm to Cluster Very Large Categorical Data Sets in Data Mining". *Cooperative Research Centre for Advanced Computational Systems*, 1997.

[Inse 00] A. Inselberg and T. Avidan. "Classification and Visualization for High-Dimensional Data". In: *Proceedings of the sixth ACM SIGKDD international conference on Knowledge discovery and data mining KDD '00*, 2000.

[Inse 05] A. Inselberg. "Visualization and Data Mining for high Dimensional Datasets". *The Data Mining and Knowledge Discovery Handbook*, pp. 297–319, 2005.

REFERENCES

[Inse 87] A. Inselberg, M. Reif, and T. Chomut. "Convexity algorithms in parallel coordinates". *Journal of the ACM (JACM)*, 1987.

[Inse 90] A. Inselberg and B. Dimsdale. "Parallel coordinates: a tool for visualizing multi-dimensional geometry". In: *Proceedings of the 1st conference on Visualization '90*, 1990.

[Jain 88] A. K. Jain and R. C. Dubes. *Algorithms for clustering data*. Prentice-Hall, Inc., Upper Saddle River, NJ, USA, 1988.

[Jain 99] A. K. Jain, M. N. Murty, and P. J. Flynn. "Data clustering: a review". *ACM Comput. Surv.*, Vol. 31, No. 3, pp. 264–323, Sep. 1999.

[Kola 06] M. Kolac. *Algorithmen für Subspace Clustering: Analyse und Vergleich*. Master's thesis, Heinrich Heine Universität Düsseldorf, 2006. 19, 123

[Krie 09] H.-P. Kriegel, P. Kröger, and A. Zimek. "Clustering high-dimensional data: A survey on subspace clustering, pattern-based clustering, and correlation clustering". *ACM Transactions on Knowledge Discovery from Data*, Vol. 3, pp. 1:1–1:58, 2009. 16, 17

[Krog 04] P. Kröger, H.-P. Kriegel, and K. Kailing. "Density-Connected Subspace Clustering for High-Dimensional Data". In: *Proc. SIAM Int. Conf. on Data Mining (SDM'04)*, pp. 246–257, 2004. 21, 97

[Li 07] J. Li, S. Ray, and B. G. Lindsay. "A Nonparametric Statistical Approach to Clustering via Mode Identification". *J. Mach. Learn. Res.*, Vol. 8, pp. 1687–1723, Dec. 2007.

REFERENCES

[Liu 00] B. Liu, Y. Xia, and P. S. Yu. "Clustering through decision tree construction". In: *Proceedings of the ninth international conference on Information and Knowledge Management*, pp. 20–29, ACM, 2000. 16

[Liu 07] G. Liu, J. Li, K. Sim, and L. Wong. "Distance Based Subspace Clustering with Flexible Dimension Partitioning". *Data Engineering, International Conference on*, Vol. 0, pp. 1250–1254, 2007. 20

[MacQ 67] J. B. MacQueen. "Some Methods for Classification and Analysis of MultiVariate Observations". In: *Proc. of the fifth Berkeley Symposium on Mathematical Statistics and Probability*, pp. 281–297, University of California Press, 1967. 14

[Maim 05] O. Maimon and L. Rokach. *The Data Mining and Knowledge Discovery Handbook*. Springer Science+Business Media, Inc., 2005.

[McQu 60] L. L. McQuitty. "Hierarchical linkage analysis for the isolation of types". *Educational and Psychological Measurement*, Vol. 20, No. 1, pp. 55–67, 1960. 16

[Mirz 08] A. Mirzaei, M. Rahmati, and M. Ahmadi. "A new method for hierarchical clustering combination". *Intell. Data Anal.*, Vol. 12, No. 6, pp. 549–571, Dec. 2008.

[Mois 08] G. Moise and J. Sander. "Finding non-redundant, statistically significant regions in high dimensional data: a novel approach to projected and subspace clustering". In: *Proceedings of the 14th ACM SIGKDD international conference on Knowledge discovery and data mining*, pp. 533–541, ACM, New York, NY, USA, 2008.

REFERENCES

[Mole 97] G. Molenberghs and E. Lesaffre. "Non-linear integral equations to construct bivariate densities with given marginals and dependence function". *Statistica Sinica*, pp. 713–738, 1997.

[Mous 02] R. E. A. Moustafa and E. J. Wegman. "On Some Generalizations of Parallel Coordinate Plots". *Center for Computational Statistics, George Mason University, Fairfax, VA, USA*, 2002.

[Mull 08] E. Müller, I. Assent, R. Krieger, T. Jansen, and T. Seidl. "Morpheus: interactive exploration of subspace clustering". In: *Proceedings of the 14th ACM SIGKDD international conference on Knowledge discovery and data mining*, pp. 1089–1092, ACM, New York, NY, USA, 2008.

[Mull 09] E. Müller, S. Günnemann, I. Assent, and T. Seidl. "Evaluating clustering in subspace projections of high dimensional data". *Proceedings of the VLDB Endowment*, Vol. 2, No. 1, pp. 1270–1281, 2009. 17

[Newt 87] S. I. Newton. *Philosophiæ Naturalis Principia Mathematica*. first Ed., 1687. 33

[Orha 08] U. Orhan, M. Hekim, and T. Ibrikci. "Gravitational Fuzzy Clustering". In: *Proceedings of the 7th Mexican International Conference on Artificial Intelligence: Advances in Artificial Intelligence*, pp. 524–531, Springer-Verlag, Berlin, Heidelberg, 2008.

[Orla 05] R. Orlandic, Y. Lai, and W. G. Yee. "Clustering high-dimensional data using an efficient and effective data space reduction". In: *CIKM '05: Proceedings of the 14th ACM international conference*

REFERENCES

on Information and knowledge management, pp. 201–208, ACM, 2005.

[Palm 04] P. Palmerini, S. Orlando, and R. Perego. "Statistical properties of transactional databases". In: *Proceedings of the 2004 ACM symposium on Applied computing*, pp. 515–519, ACM, New York, NY, USA, 2004.

[Park 07] N. H. Park and W. S. Lee. "Grid-based subspace clustering over data streams". In: *Proceedings of the sixteenth ACM conference on Conference on information and knowledge management*, pp. 801–810, ACM, New York, NY, USA, 2007.

[Pars 04] L. Parsons, E. Haque, and H. Liu. "Subspace clustering for high dimensional data: A review". *SIGKDD Explor. Newsl.*, Vol. 6, pp. 90–105, 2004. 2, 3, 16, 123

[Patr 06] A. Patrikainen and M. Meila. "Comparing Subspace Clusterings". *IEEE Trans. on Knowl. and Data Eng.*, Vol. 18, No. 7, pp. 902–916, July 2006.

[Proc 02] C. M. Procopiuc, M. Jones, P. K. Agarwal, and T. M. Murali. "A Monte Carlo algorithm for fast projective clustering". In: *Proceedings of the 2002 ACM SIGMOD international conference on Management of data*, pp. 418–427, ACM, 2002. 16

[Robe 00] J. Roberts. "From know-how to show-how? Questioning the role of information and communication technologies in knowledge transfer". *Technology Analysis & Strategic Management*, Vol. 12, No. 4, pp. 429–443, 2000. 27

REFERENCES

[Rous 87] L. Rousseeuw and L. Kaufman. "Clustering by means of medoids". *Statistical data analysis based on the L1-norm and related methods*, Vol. 405, 1987. 15

[Shan 48] C. E. Shannon. "A mathematical theory of communication". *Bell system technical journal*, Vol. 27, pp. 379–423, 1948. 50

[Shi 03] Y. Shi, Y. Song, and A. Zhang. "A shrinking-based approach for multi-dimensional data analysis". In: *VLDB '2003: Proceedings of the 29th international conference on Very large data bases*, pp. 440–451, VLDB Endowment, 2003.

[Shi 08] Y. Shi. "FuzzyShrinking: improving shrinking-based data mining algorithms using fuzzy concept for multi-dimensional data". In: *Proceedings of the 46th Annual Southeast Regional Conference on XX*, pp. 260–263, ACM, New York, NY, USA, 2008.

[Sim 12] K. Sim, V. Gopalkrishnan, A. Zimek, and G. Cong. "A survey on enhanced subspace clustering". *Data Mining and Knowledge Discovery*, pp. 1–66, 2012. 17

[Snea 57] P. H. Sneath. "The application of computers to taxonomy". *Journal of general microbiology*, Vol. 17, No. 1, pp. 201–226, 1957. 15

[Soka 58] R. Sokal and C. Michener. "A statistical method for evaluating systematic relationships". *University of Kansas Scientific Bulletin*, Vol. 38, pp. 1409–1438, 1958. 16

[Spä 73] H. Späth. "Clustering of one-dimensional ordered data". *Computing*, Vol. 11, No. 2, pp. 175–177, 1973.

REFERENCES

[Tan 05] P.-N. Tan, M. Steinbach, and V. Kumar. *Introduction to data mining*. Addison-Wesley, 2005.

[Woo 04] K.-G. Woo, J.-H. Lee, M.-H. Kim, and Y.-J. Lee. "FINDIT: a Fast and Intelligent Subspace Clustering Algorithm using Dimension Voting". *Information and Software Technology*, Vol. 46, No. 4, pp. 255–271, 2004. 16, 23, 99

[Xu 98] X. Xu, M. Ester, H.-P. Kriegel, and J. Sander. "A Distribution-Based Clustering Algorithm for Mining in Large Spatial Databases". In: *Proceedings of the Fourteenth International Conference on Data Engineering*, pp. 324–331, IEEE Computer Society, Washington, DC, USA, 1998.

[Yang 02] J. Yang, W. Wang, H. Wang, and P. Yu. "δ-Clusters: Capturing Subspace Correlation in a Large Data Set". In: *Data Engineering, 2002. Proceedings. 18th International Conference on*, pp. 517–528, 2002. 16

[Zhan 11] X. Zhang, Y. Qiu, and Y. Wu. "Exploiting constraint inconsistence for dimension selection in subspace clustering: A semi-supervised approach". *Neurocomput.*, Vol. 74, No. 17, pp. 3598–3608, Oct. 2011.

[Zhao 09] J. Zhao. "Automatische Parameterbestimmung durch Gravitation in Subspace Clustering". *21. Workshop "Grundlagen von Datenbanken", Rostock*, 2009.

[Zhao 10a] J. Zhao. "Automatic parameter determination in subspace clustering with gravitation function". In: *Proceedings of the Fourteenth*

REFERENCES

International Database Engineering and Applications Symposium, pp. 130–135, ACM, 2010. 6, 24, 27, 33, 45, 85, 103

[Zhao 10b] J. Zhao. "Subspace Clustering with Gravitation". *Proceedings of the 22nd Workshop "Grundlagen von Datenbanken 2010"*, Bad Helmstedt, Germany, 2010.

[Zhao 12] J. Zhao and S. Conrad. "Automatic Subspace Clustering with Density Function". In: *International Confenrence on Data Technologies and Applications*, pp. 63–69, SciTePress Digital Library, 2012. 6, 24, 27, 85, 103

[Zhao 13] J. Zhao and S. Conrad. "Subspace Clustering with Distance-Density Function and Entropy in High-Dimensional Data". In: *International Confenrence on Data Management Technologies and Applications*, SciTePress Digital Library, 2013. 6, 24, 27, 85, 103

REFERENCES

LIST OF FIGURES

1.1	An example of "curse of dimensionality" [Pars 04]	3
1.2	An example of subspace clusters	4
2.1	DBSCAN with $minPts = 5$	10
2.2	Density values of DENCLUE with different σ [Hinn 98]	12
2.3	Clustering results of DENCLUE with different ξ [Hinn 98]	13
2.4	Dense units in CLIQUE [Kola 06]	19
3.1	Evenly distributed objects and cluster objects	32
3.2	An illustration of gravitation in a one-dimensional subspace	35
3.3	An illustration of gravitation with evenly distributed objects	36
3.4	An example of clusters selection in SUGRA	41
3.5	An example of SUGRA in two-dimensional data set	44
3.6	An example of the distance-density function of ASCDD	47
3.7	An example of the distance-density for a two-dimensional subspace with ASCDD	48
3.8	An example of distance-density of evenly distributed objects with ASCDD	49
3.9	An example of detecting a potential subspace	54
3.10	Distance-density of objects in the subspace {x,y}	55
3.11	Neighboring objects	57
3.12	An example of $T_{min}^{\tilde{A}}$ and $T_{max}^{\tilde{A}}$	61
3.13	An example of clustering process of ASCDD	62
4.1	Gravitation values with different scales of data	68

LIST OF FIGURES

4.2	An example of concave clusters	69
4.3	Density of objects and clustering result with $q = 0$	70
4.4	Clustering result with $q = 0.1$ and $q = 0.2$	71
4.5	Clustering result with $q = 0.3$ and $q = 0.4$	71
4.6	Clustering result with $q = 0.5$ and $q = 0.6$	72
4.7	Clustering result with $q = 0.7$ and $q = 0.8$	72
4.8	Clustering result with $q = 0.9$ and $q = 1$	73
4.9	An example of two-dimensional concave clusters	74
4.10	Density values of concave clusters	75
4.11	Clustering result with ASCDD	75
4.12	Comparison of clustering results with SUGRA and ASCDD	77
4.13	Comparison of clustering results with SUGRA and CLIQUE	78
4.14	Comparison of ASCDD and DENCLUE	80
5.1	Run time (Objects) (SUGRA vs. CLIQUE)	87
5.2	Run time (Dimension) (SUGRA vs. CLIQUE)	87
5.3	Gravitation of the four attributes on "iris"	90
5.4	Clustering result of "Galaxy" with ASCDD	93
5.5	Clustering result of "Galaxy" with ASCDD demonstrated in 3D	94
5.6	Run time with different q	95
5.7	ASCDD compared with ENCLUS	96

LIST OF TABLES

3.1	Table structure of a data set	29
3.2	Gravitation threshold with different number of objects	37
4.1	An example of entropy values calculated with ENCLUS	81
4.2	An example of entropy values calculated with ASCDD	82
5.1	Comparison of clustering results from SUGRA and CLIQUE	88
5.2	Accuracy of SUGRA on "iris"	89
5.3	Threshold setting for SUGRA on "wine"	91
5.4	Result of ASCDD on "wine"	99
5.5	Results of ASCDD and ENCLUS on "Gas Sensor Array Drift"	101
7.1	A three dimensional data set	108

LIST OF TABLES

INDEX

ε-neighborhood, 10

Anomaly detection, 2
ASCDD, 45
Association rule mining, 2
Attribute, 28
Average distance, 40
Average-Link, 16

Bottom-up, 16

CBF, 20
Classification, 1
CLIQUE, 18
Cluster, 2
Cluster objects, 38
Clustering, 2
Complete-Link, 16
Concave shaped cluster, 73
Convex shaped cluster, 73
Coverage, 19
Curse of dimensionality, 3, 31

Data, 27
Data set, 28
Data type, 27

DBSCAN, 9
DENCLUE, 12
Dense area, 32
Density-connected, 10
Density-reachable, 10
Dimension, 28
Directly density-reachable, 10
Distance-density, 46
Distance-Density Threshold DDT, 59
Downward-closure, 17

ENCLUS, 19
Entropy, 19, 50
Euclidean distance, 30
Euclidean space, 30
Evenly distribution, 31
Expectation-Maximization, 12
Expression level, 5

FINDIT, 23
Fuzzy C-Means, 15

Gaussian kernel function, 12
Gravitation, 33
Gravitation threshold $\overline{G^a}$, 36
Gravitational constant, 33

INDEX

Hill-climbing, 13

Interest, 20
Interest gain, 20
Intersection, 30

k-Means, 14
k-medoids, 15

MAFIA, 20
Maximal dimensionality, 53
Medoid, 15
Monotonicity, 17

nCluster, 20
Neighborhood, 60
Non-cluster objects, 40
Normalized entropy, 51

Object, 28
ORCLUS, 22

PreDeCon, 21
Probability, 51
PROCLUS, 22

Regression analysis, 1
Relational database, 28

Set of neighbors, 58
Similarity, 2

Single-Link, 15
Standard deviation, 12
Start object, 60
SUBCLU, 21
Subspace, 4, 28
Subspace cluster, 29
Subspace clustering, 3, 16
   density-based, 20
   grid-based, 18
   partition-based, 22
Subspace clustering result, 30
SUGRA, 33

Table, 28
Top-down, 16
Traditional clustering, 2
Traditional clustering, 9
   density-based, 9
   hierarchy-based, 15
   partition-based, 14
   statistics-based, 11
Tuple, 28

i want morebooks!

Buy your books fast and straightforward online - at one of world's fastest growing online book stores! Environmentally sound due to Print-on-Demand technologies.

Buy your books online at
www.get-morebooks.com

Kaufen Sie Ihre Bücher schnell und unkompliziert online – auf einer der am schnellsten wachsenden Buchhandelsplattformen weltweit! Dank Print-On-Demand umwelt- und ressourcenschonend produziert.

Bücher schneller online kaufen
www.morebooks.de

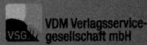 VDM Verlagsservicegesellschaft mbH
Heinrich-Böcking-Str. 6-8   Telefon: +49 681 3720 174   info@vdm-vsg.de
D - 66121 Saarbrücken   Telefax: +49 681 3720 1749   www.vdm-vsg.de

Printed by Books on Demand GmbH, Norderstedt / Germany